JESUS
OF NAZARETH

JESUS
OF NAZARETH

William Barclay

based on the film directed by Franco Zeffirelli
from the script by Anthony Burgess, Suso Cecchi d'Amico
and Franco Zeffirelli

Photographs by Paul Ronald

COLLINS + WORLD
London · Glasgow · Cleveland
1977

First published 1977
© RAI   I.T.C. Entertainment Limited
and William Barclay, 1977

ISBN 0 00 250653 X

Set in 'Monophoto' Apollo by
Filmtype Services, Scarborough and
Art Reprographic, London
Colour separations by Gilchrist Bros, Leeds
Made and printed in Great Britain by
William Collins Sons & Co. Ltd, Glasgow

CONTENTS

INTRODUCTION

This book is based on Anthony Burgess' script of the film *Jesus of Nazareth*. The script of the film was in my hands when I wrote it, and there are large areas of the book where I did no more than change the script into narrative form.

It may well be that there are some who think it is an irreverence to make the life of Jesus into a film, but there are fewer and fewer people who read and more and more who learn by looking at pictures. I therefore regard the writing of this book as an opportunity to be seized.

Every generation has its own method of learning. For long, the method of learning in the English-speaking countries has been by way of the book and the written word. More and more this has been changing until the method of learning has been through the picture. This book will bring the life of Jesus into the lives of many, which could not have been brought in in any other way. The eye-gate to learning has always been stronger than the ear-gate, and this film has been designed to appeal to the eye-gate through the remarkable film stills which accompany the text.

In the film and in this book the story of Jesus is told simply and straight-forwardly. There is no attempt at sensationalism. The story, in all its simplicity, is allowed to make its own impact. It may well be that the seeing of this film may send viewers back to the gospels themselves, and if they do go back to the gospels, they will read them with a new intelligence and a new vividness after seeing this film. It is our hope that this book may enable ordinary people to see Jesus more vividly and may move them to commit their lives to him.

William Barclay

PART 1

THE COMING

PHOTOGRAPHS

Although only a small town in a tiny province Nazareth was far from being remote. Traffic from the ends of the earth passed close to its borders. A boy had only to climb the hill at the back of the town to see the Road of the Sea which came up from Egypt and went out to Damascus, along which the great trading caravans with their strings of laden camels moved constantly. He would see also the Road of the East running from the Mediterranean to Parthia and beyond, along which trading adventurers passed to remote lands, and the Roman legions clanked their way to service on the eastern frontiers of the Empire. He had only to look westward and the blue waters of the Mediterranean lay shimmering before him, dotted with ships sailing to Egypt, to Greece and to Rome.

While its situation encouraged the youth of Nazareth to dream of far away places, political conditions excited their elders, like Jews everywhere, to dream of the future – of a Golden Age when all the world would bow to the coming Jewish Messiah. The dreams varied strangely, however. Some were of a worldwide Empire under a conquering Messiah who would impose his will by force. Others were of a universal rule founded on love and truth, to which all would freely and joyfully assent. And while many dreamed, there were some who plotted direct action here and now to cast off the Roman yoke.

Discussions about the future went on everywhere including the house of Yehuda the Rabbi. There were sceptics, like Jotham, who had lost faith in messianic dreams. The prophets had long been dead, and their unfulfilled predictions had become mere irrelevances. But a future without hope, said the Rabbi, was like a night without stars; and he reminded them of the signs that would herald the dawn of the new age, 'then the eyes of the blind shall be opened, and the ears of the deaf unstopped; then shall the lame man leap as an hart, and the tongue of the dumb sing for joy', and there was that greatest sign of all: 'A virgin shall conceive and bear a son'.

Herod the Great ruled in Palestine when Jesus was born. In many ways a great king he was driven almost mad by fear of treachery from those close to the throne, and his insane suspicions of his nearest and dearest impelled him to murder his wife Asariamme, her mother Alexandra, his sons Alexander, Aristobulus and Antipater. As Augustus the Roman Emperor, making a play on the Greek words, cynically remarked, it was safer to be Herod's *hus* (pig) than to be his *huros* (son).

Herod ruled by permission of Rome and as a consequence was hated by the Jews, who despised him also since he was half Idumaean. He tried, unsuccessfully, to win popular favour by a lavish rebuilding of the Jewish temple. But he would tolerate no intrusion of religion into politics, and any man with claims to being a prophet was closely watched. So long as his message was non-political he was left alone, but if the righteousness he proclaimed acquired a political connotation he was effectively silenced, if necessary by being killed. Anyone with the remotest claim to being Messiah was eliminated, for the last thing Herod wanted was a rebellion against Rome, which would cost him his throne.

There was a devout family living in Nazareth during Herod's reign, the head of which, Joachin, died, leaving Anna his widow with only a daughter, Mary, who was engaged to marry Joseph, the village carpenter. As a carpenter Joseph was a craftsman of some standing, and he came of a distinguished family, for he was a direct descendant of King David.

Then to Mary's astonishment and no small dread, the angel Gabriel appeared to her, bringing a message from God. 'Joy be with you!' he said. 'You are specially dear to God! The Lord is with you!' She was deeply moved at what he said, and wondered what a greeting like this could mean. 'Don't be afraid, Mary,' the angel said to her, 'God has chosen you for a very precious privilege. You will conceive, and you will have a son, and you must give him the name Jesus. He will be great; his title will be "the Son of the Most High". The Lord will give him the throne of David his ancestor. He will reign over the house of Jacob for ever, and his reign will never come to an end.' Mary said to the angel, 'How can this happen when I have no husband?' The angel answered, 'The Holy Spirit will come upon you, and the power of the Most High will overshadow you. That is why the holy child who will be born will be called Son of God. Elisabeth, your kinswoman, has also conceived a son in her old age. They said that she could never have a child. But now she is in her sixth month, for there is nothing impossible to God.' Mary said, 'I am the Lord's servant. Whatever you say, I accept.' And the angel went away and left her.

In this way Mary learnt that she was to have a child without human paternity, who would be the Messiah.

She had already heard the remarkable news of her kinswoman, Elisabeth, who was pregnant although long past the age of child-bearing; and she at once decided to set out for the small Judean town where Elisabeth lived and visit her. When she arrived the baby stirred in Elisabeth's womb, and Elisabeth burst into inspired speech:

'You are the most blessed of women and blessed is the child you will bear. Why have I received this privilege that the mother of my Lord should come to me? For, when I heard your greeting, the baby in my womb leaped for joy. Blessed is she who has believed that the message she received from the Lord will come true.'

And Mary answered:
'My soul tells me of the greatness of God,
   and my spirit thrills in God my Saviour,
   because he has looked kindly on his servant,
   even though my place in life is humble.

From now on those of all time to come will call me blessed,
  for the Mighty One has done great things for me,
  and holy is his name.
His mercy is from age to age
  to those who reverence him.
He has done mighty deeds with his right arm.
He has scattered the proud with their arrogant plans.
He has thrown down the mighty from their seats of power.
He has exalted the humble,
He has filled those who are hungry with good things,
  and those who are rich he has sent empty away.
He has come to the aid of Israel his servant.
He has kept the promise that he made to our fathers,
  the promise never to forget his mercy to Abraham,
  and to his descendants for ever.'

Mary stayed with Elisabeth for three months and then returned home. Her personal problem was then inescapable. She had to tell her mother and Joseph that she was carrying a child which had been conceived without intercourse. Joseph, unable to credit her story, was heartbroken. He consulted with the village rabbi, who could do no better than quote the Law to him, which left him no option but to annul the marriage contract. He was anxious not to shame Mary publicly, however, and planned to divorce her in secret. At this pass he too received a message from God. It reached him through a dream in which the angel of the Lord appeared and spoke to him.

'Joseph, son of David,' the angel said, 'do not hesitate to marry Mary, for it is as a result of the action of the Holy Spirit that she is going to have a child. She will have a son, and you must call him by the name Jesus, for it is he who will save his people from their sins.' All this happened that the statement made by the Lord through the prophet might come true:

'The virgin shall conceive and have a child,
and they shall give him the name Emmanuel'

for that name means 'God is with us'. So Joseph woke from sleep and carried out the instructions of the angel of the Lord. He married Mary and she had her son. And they called him by the name Jesus.

So Joseph believed that Mary had spoken the truth, and they were married.

As the time for the child's birth drew near, Rome decreed that a census of the whole Empire must be taken. The decree was highly unpopular, for it was common knowledge that censuses were taken to determine the number of men liable for military service, and to bring the registers relating to taxation up to date.

To the Jews a census was particularly obnoxious, for their religious traditions were against it, and a census imposed by a foreign power mocked their most sacred principle: 'No rule but the Lord, no King but God.' To prevent violent outbursts while the census was being taken, the Romans therefore ordered each man to be registered, not at his place of residence, but at the headquarters of his clan or tribe. In this way dangerous combinations of the rebellious might be avoided, for while a man could trust friends and neighbours of his home town, he would be cautious about plotting with strangers.

The conditions of the census thus forced Joseph to travel from his home in Nazareth to Bethlehem, the ancestral town of David, to whose family he belonged. Mary would have to travel with him, and when they were due to depart the time for Mary's delivery would be so near that her child was virtually certain to be born in Bethlehem. Realizing this, Joseph was astonished and deeply moved, for he remembered the prophecy of Micah: 'But thou, O Bethlehem, from you shall come forth for me one who is to be ruler of Israel'. Thus by reason of the census Mary's baby would be delivered in the very town which prophecy identified as the birthplace of the Messiah. Any last lingering doubts Joseph retained about Mary's astonishing story were swept away, and he wholly and joyfully believed.

For Mary the long journey to Bethlehem was exhausting, and they arrived to find the inns so crowded that Joseph could secure no accommodation for her. But at one place where they were turned away, a serving girl, distressed by Mary's condition, told them of a stable where they could find shelter. It would at least be warm and dry. Mary's need was then so acute that they gratefully accepted the girl's suggestion, and it was in a stable that Mary was delivered and Jesus was born.

It was not long before the newly-born infant had his first visitors. During the night hours some shepherds were in the fields outside Bethlehem keeping watch over their sheep. The guard was needed against human as much as animal predators, for the great influx of visitors to Bethlehem had raised food prices and increased the value of sheep. The shepherds were doubtless themselves hoping to sell their lambs at a very high price. They were rough men, but like peasants everywhere they were shrewd. It was to these men that God's messenger Gabriel also appeared. Thus Luke tells the story:

'In that district there were shepherds out in the fields, guarding their flock by night. An angel of the Lord appeared to them, and the glory of the Lord shone round them, and they were terrified. "Don't be afraid," the angel said to them, "for I am bringing you good news of great joy, a joy in which all peoples will share. For today there has been born to you in David's town a saviour who is the Messiah, the Lord. This is how you will recognize him. You will find a baby, wrapped in swaddling clothes, lying in a manger." Suddenly there was with the angel a crowd of heaven's army, singing God's praise. "Glory to God in the heights of heaven," they sang, "and on earth peace to mankind, on whom God's favour rests".'

When the angels had left them and returned to heaven, the shepherds exclaimed 'What wonders of God are these!' And one said, 'Come! we must risk leaving the sheep. At all costs we must go to Bethlehem and see the child the angels have told us about.' So they hurried to the town as fast as their legs would carry them. There they found Mary and Joseph with the baby lying in the manger, as the angels had said.

When they came away they could not contain themselves, but told everyone they met of their wonderful experience. Those who heard of it were astonished and told others, and so the story was spread about. The shepherds then went back to their sheep glorifying and praising God for all that they had heard and seen. And Mary treasured the memory of their coming, wondering at all that was happening.

20

The shepherds were not the only visitors to the stable. Others, strangely different, were coming a long way to find him. Caspar, Melchior and Balthasar were magi from the East, men of great learning who studied the night sky in their own separate countries, believing they could read in the stars predictions of future events on earth. In the year Jesus was born the planets Jupiter and Saturn met in the sign of the zodiac called Pisces, the Fish. The conjunction takes place only once every 794 years, and it is a brilliant sight. The magi held Pisces to be the sign of *the last days*; Jupiter they regarded as the star of *the world ruler*; while Saturn was *the star of Palestine*. They therefore reckoned that when Jupiter met Saturn in the constellation of Pisces, the ruler of the last days would appear in Palestine; and they travelled to Palestine to find him, bringing him gifts.

Before they could find Jesus the story of their coming reached Herod. When he learnt that they had come to find a new king his suspicious fears were at once aroused, and he intended to murder the child who would, as he thought, be a threat to his own power.

In due time the baby Jesus was brought to the synagogue to be circumcised. There was present in the synagogue an aged saint named Simeon, who 'meticulously observed the Law and devoutly reverenced God,' as St Luke says, and who had become assured through the Holy Spirit 'that death would not come to him until he had seen the Lord's Messiah'. When he saw Jesus he took him in his arms and said:

'Now, O Lord, as you promised,
you are giving your servant his release in peace,
because my eyes have seen the saving power
which you have prepared for all peoples to see,
to be a light to bring your revelation to the Gentiles,
and glory to your people Israel.'

Mary and Joseph returned with Jesus to the stable and there found the three magi waiting for them with their gifts of gold, frankincense and myrrh.

The magi, who had learnt about Herod's real purpose, warned Mary and Joseph to leave Palestine and they accordingly took the baby Jesus and set out on the long road to Egypt. The magi, to evade Herod, meanwhile returned to their own lands by another route. When he realized that he had been tricked Herod's rage knew no bounds, and he ordered the slaughter of every male child in Bethlehem up to the age of two.

4

6

27

PART 2

PREPARING
THE WAY

PHOTOGRAPHS

In due time Herod the Great died, and his death presented the Romans with a problem. Whatever the Jews thought about him, from the standpoint of Rome Herod was an eminently satisfactory ruler, who had succeeded in keeping Palestine quiet and trouble-free. None of his sons had inherited his ability as a ruler, however, and Augustus decided to split Palestine between the three of them. Judea was entrusted to Archelaus despite the fact that he was so unpopular with the Jews that they sent an Embassy to Rome requesting that Philip, the best of the sons, was given Ituraea. Galilee was handed over to Herod Antipas, whom Jesus was to call 'that fox'.

In due time news of Herod's death and the redistribution of his Kingdom reached Egypt. When Joseph heard about it he immediately made preparations to return home, although he was warned to avoid Jerusalem which was wracked with troubles under the unsatisfactory Archelaus.

Joseph and Mary thus returned to Palestine. Anna was dead, but there were many to give them an astonished welcome, having never thought to see them again. They took over Anna's house and Joseph got the carpenter's shop going again. Meanwhile Archelaus had made such a mess of things in Judea that the Romans finally exiled him, and replaced him with a Roman procurator whose headquarters were in Caesarea on the sea coast.

Even in Nazareth the new political set-up made itself felt. There was, for instance, the day when a squadron of Roman cavalry, on its way from Damascus to Jerusalem, appeared in the village and proceeded to seize everything eatable. Reminded that Nazareth was in Galilee, and Galilee was not under direct Roman rule, they answered that an army on the road must eat, and added proudly that as far as they were concerned the whole world was Rome.

Such conduct gave great offence to all, but it enraged the Zealots, a party whose name signified their zeal for the Jewish law. So fanatical were they that when a law was broken they were prepared to murder the offender, be he Jew or Gentile. Believing the Jews should acknowledge no king but God, they longed and schemed for the day when they would be strong enough to make a successful armed rebellion against the hated Romans.

Always on the verge of revolt, seeking all the time for a leader who could carry them to victory, when an incident like the soldiers' raid on Nazareth occurred the younger Zealots in particular were hard to control.

Meanwhile the boy Jesus was growing up. He played in the carpenter's shop and would sometimes climb a ladder Joseph was making to see the roads going north, south and east, and glimpse the sparkle of the blue waters of the Mediterranean away to the west: and dreams of a world would fill his mind.

He attended the village school where Rabbi Yehuda taught. One day the Rabbi was giving the class a test in unseen reading. He handed a scroll to the boys one after another, but they could make nothing of it. Then came the turn of Jesus. Clearly and easily Jesus read:

The Lord is my shepherd. He leadeth me to green pastures, and maketh me to lie by the quiet waters.

The Rabbi was deeply impressed by the boy's progress. 'And do you know who wrote it?' he asked. 'My great, great, great, great, great, great grandfather, King David,' he answered. Jesus knew his ancestry even as a boy.

The day came when he officially 'grew up'. In Palestine, a boy became a man on his twelfth birthday. From that time onwards he was personally responsible for keeping the law: he was eligible to be a witness in a law-court; he could take part in the reading of the Scripture Lesson and the discussion in the synagogue. A ceremony initiating the boy into becoming *Bar Mitzwah*, a son of the law, was held in the synagogue. It continues among the Jews to this day, and part of the prayer which the boy prays is as follows:

O my God and God of my fathers, on this solemn and sacred day, which marks my passage from boyhood to manhood, I humbly raise my eyes unto thee, and declare with sincerity and truth, that henceforth I will keep thy commandments, and undertake and bear the responsibility of my actions towards thee. In my earliest infancy I was brought within thy sacred covenant with Israel: and today I again enter, as an active responsible member, into this elect congregation, in the midst of which I will never cease to proclaim thy holy name in the face of all nations.

Doubtless Jesus used the prayer on the day he became a *Bar Mitzwah* in the Synagogue in Nazareth.

Having become officially an adult, Jesus had to fulfil certain religious duties. Every adult male Jew was obliged to attend three annual festivals at Jerusalem: Passover, Pentecost and Tabernacles. Greatest of all was the Passover, for which the most careful preparation had to be made. For six weeks, as the time for it approached, it was the subject of sermons in the synagogue and lessons in school. Like other Jewish boys, Jesus prepared to attend his first Passover.

Jerusalem was a hundred miles from Nazareth, and the caravan from the village, slow-moving for the sake of mothers and children, took about a week on the journey.

What a thrill it was when the Temple came in sight! Josephus describes its dazzling appearance: 'The outward face of the Temple in its front wanted nothing that was likely either to surprise men's minds or their eyes; for it was covered all over with plates of gold of great weight and, at the first rising of the sun reflected back a very fiery splendour and made those who forced themselves to look upon it to turn away their eyes, just as they would at the sun's own rays. The Temple appeared to strangers when they were at a distance like the mountain covered with snow, for those parts of it which were not gilt were exceedingly white.' As they marched on their way, and especially as they were climbing Mount Sion to the sacred city, the pilgrims sang what the English Bible calls 'The Songs of Ascents', Psalms 120–134. 'I was glad when they said to me, Let us go into the house of the Lord!'

What would Jesus see when he came into Jerusalem for the first time? As he came to the city gates he would see both sides of the road lined with scaffolds for those who were to be executed. Next, the Temple. He would be instructed beforehand as to its layout, but it was built in a series of courts. The outermost was the Court of the Gentiles, into which anyone might come but beyond which no Gentile must pass. Next was the Court of the Women, into which all Jews could enter but beyond which no woman must go. Then came the Court of the Israelites, beyond which no layman must venture. Finally there was the Court of the Priests, with the great altar and, at the far end, the Holy Place and the Holy of Holies, which no one might enter except the High Priest, and he only once a year on the Day of Atonement.

The Court of the Gentiles presented an extraordinary spectacle. In it the merchants who sold pigeons and lambs for the sacrifices had their shops, and the money-changers had their tables. The place was like a busy market rather than part of the Temple.

The main part of the Passover Meal was the lamb. It commemorated the deliverance from Egypt, when a last terrible plague broke Pharaoh's resistance and he allowed the Israelites to depart. An angel of death was to pass through the land and slay the first-born son in every Egyptian household. To keep their own homes unscathed the Israelites were instructed to mark the lintel of their doorposts with the blood of a lamb, and the avenging angel would *pass over* the houses so marked. The Passover Feast was eaten in the evening in the homes of the people, but before that, the lamb, which was the main part of the feast, had first to be offered in the Temple. The blood of the animal was sacred to God, for the Jews identified the blood with the life. The lamb had therefore to be slaughtered by a priest and its blood poured on to the altar. Something of what the Temple courts must have been like can be gauged from the fact that a census of lambs slain at the Passover of year 65, when Cestius Gallus was governor, established a figure of 256,500 animals sacrificed in that one year alone. It baffles the imagination to think what the altar must have been like after the blood of more than a quarter of a million lambs had been poured on it. The number of lambs gives us an idea of the number of people in Jerusalem at Passover time. A Passover house gathering had to consist of a minimum of ten people to each lamb. This means that well over 2,565,000 were packed into Jerusalem at Passover time.

It was Jesus who was holding in his arms the lamb which the group from Nazareth wished sacrificed. He handed over the lamb with a look of intense sorrow in his eyes. In his heart he seemed to be sharing the tragedy of the lamb, while a Levite's voice was repeating Isaiah's famous words:

He was despised and rejected of men; a man of sorrows and acquainted with grief; and we hid as it were our faces from him; he was despised and we esteemed him not. Surely he has borne our griefs and carried our sorrow; yet we did esteem him stricken, smitten of God, and afflicted.

All we like sheep have gone astray; we have turned every one to his own way; and the Lord has laid on him the iniquity of us all. He was oppressed and he was afflicted, yet he opened not his mouth; he is brought as a lamb to the slaughter, and as a sheep before her shearers is dumb so he openeth not his mouth.

He was wounded for our transgressions, he was bruised for our iniquities; the chastisement of our peace was upon him; and with his stripes we are healed.

When the lamb was handed back to be the Passover Meal, its body was slit down the middle and kept open by two pieces of wood – in the form of a cross.

The lamb slain, the cross of wood, the words from Isaiah – hints of his destiny were beginning to enter the mind of the boy Jesus.

So the ancient ritual unfolded. It was partly memory of the past:

O Lord, thou hast given us this day of the Passover that we may re-live our exodus. Glory to thee, O Lord, who blessest Israel and the feasts thereof.

It was partly hope for the future:

This is the bread of affliction that our fathers ate in the land of Egypt. He who hungers, let him come and eat with us. This night we are in bondage; tomorrow we shall be free.

In this way they remembered the day when God had delivered them from bondage in Egypt, and hoped for the day when God would deliver them from bondage to Rome.

The time came for Joseph and Mary to set out with the caravan on the return journey to Nazareth. The women left first because they walked more slowly. The men followed later. The men caught up and they were all together at the evening halting place. It was then that Mary and Joseph discovered that Jesus was not with them. Up to that time neither had worried, because Mary had thought that he was with Joseph and Joseph supposed that he was with his mother. They hurried to the caravan master who told them that he must be with the other children in the centre of the caravan; but Jesus was not there. There was nothing for it, they must go back to Jerusalem and look for him.

What had Jesus been doing in his time alone in Jerusalem? He had seen the women of the streets flirt with the Roman soldiers. He had seen criminals being led to the place of execution, carrying the cross-piece of the gibbets to which they would be nailed. As he watched, someone in the crowd quoted scripture: 'Cursed be he who hangs from the wood of the tree'.

With sinking hearts Joseph and Mary searched all through the streets of Jerusalem, but they could not find him. At last they turned their footsteps to the Temple. The Sanhedrin, the supreme court of Jews which settled all points of faith and doctrine, ethics and law, was in session. Normally it met in private but during Passover time it met publicly in the Temple colonnades. Its arguments and discussions for this one week were open to all. And it was there that Joseph and Mary found Jesus, young as he was, listening to the members of the Sanhedrin, speaking and asking them questions, taking a full part in the discussions. Mary went to Jesus. 'Son,' she said, 'why did you do this to us? Your father and I have been searching everywhere for you, and we have been desperately worried.'

'Did you not know,' said Jesus, 'that I must be in my Father's house?'

5

6

When Jesus was thirty years old, John the Baptist suddenly emerged on the national scene. John was a child of the desert. He had gone into the wilderness, far from cities and their thronging crowds, and in rugged solitude had lived close to nature, near to God. Suddenly he issued a prophetic call, startling in its passion and conviction, for a return to righteousness. People streamed out to the place by the Jordan where he preached, and hundreds responded to his call and were baptized in the river in token of repentance from their sins.

National groups reacted to him in differing ways. While the Zealots saw him as a potential rabble-rouser, and wanted to use him for their cause, the Pharisees resented his searing call to repentance. Were they not sons of Abraham? And did not descent from Abraham guarantee salvation? They even had a saying that God had stationed an angel at the mouth of hell to turn back any descendant of Abraham who mistakenly arrived there. John told them that God could, if he chose, turn the very stones of the desert into sons of Abraham. What mattered was not a man's ancestry but his own living, the way he treated his fellow men.

The Sadducees, who had control of the priesthood and the Temple, were incensed by an unofficial religious movement. They sent to ask John who he thought he was and where he got his authority. John answered that his authority was from God, and that he was a forerunner of one whose very sandal he was not worthy to untie, and who would baptize them not with water but with the Holy Spirit and with fire.

By this time Joseph had died. He was sad to leave Mary, for he knew that Jesus would not remain with her much longer. 'We have always known,' he said 'that it was not for us that he came to earth.' So he died, whispering with his last breath, as Jesus was also one day to do, 'Into thy hands I commend my spirit'.

News of John's crusade was the signal for Jesus to leave home. He went with the crowds to hear John preach, and presented himself for baptism in the river. John had a sudden flash of recognition and said, 'It is I who should be baptized by you, and yet you come to me'. Jesus raised him up. 'Let it be so,' he said, 'it is only right for us to do everything a good man ought to do.' John then consented to baptize Jesus, and there came a voice from heaven: 'This is my son, the beloved, the only one, in whom I am well pleased'.

With his baptism something momentous happened to Jesus. He knew that for him the hour had struck. He must begin the work for which he had come into the world. But how was he to proceed? He had to gain the attention of men and then to win their allegiance. There were alternative methods he could use, and it would be fatally easy to choose the wrong way. He therefore went out into the wilderness to reflect over the alternatives, and reject alluring short-cuts. As the gospels put it, he went into the desert

to be tempted of the Devil. We must not think of the conflict happening, as it were, visibly. The whole struggle went on in the mind of Jesus. Nor must we think of the temptations proceeding in three distinct acts. The struggle was being waged in the mind of Jesus all the forty days he was in the wilderness.

The first temptation arose when he was feeling tired and hungry and very much alone. Stones looking like small loaves covered the ground. Conscious of his superhuman power, Jesus felt an impulse to turn the stones into bread. 'Use your powers for your own comfort and security,' the Tempter was inwardly saying to him. But Jesus refused. 'It takes more than bread to keep a man alive,' he answered, 'man lives by every word that comes out of the mouth of God.'

The second temptation was more subtle. 'Look,' whispered the Tempter, 'how can you expect anyone to believe in you? You, an unknown carpenter from Nazareth! Startle them into paying attention. Get God to work a spectacular miracle for you. Jump off the highest spire of the Temple and float down and land unharmed. That will impress the people and they will assuredly follow you.' But Jesus refused to use the power of God for magical displays. 'You must never try,' he said 'to see how far you can go with God and get away with it.'

In the third temptation the inner voice said, 'Think of the poor, the enslaved, the deprived, the suffering. They wait for your coming and desperately need your help. You will be unable to tackle a problem so vast and bring them relief, unless you have *power*. Follow my way and I will give you mastery over the whole earth.' Here the temptation was to compromise, to seek first the visible power and glory of this world. But again Jesus refused. He had come not to be served but to serve, and he must serve God alone if he was to bring to men the help they so desperately needed.

Thus Jesus conquered the Tempter, and when day broke and morning came he left the desert, his mind made up, and returned to mingle again with men.

11

16

PART 3

FISHER OF MEN

PHOTOGRAPHS

1 At first there was a shocked silence and
   then the congregation began to buzz with
   discontent

2 In the roadway outside the synagogue the men
   of the village resolved to make an example of
   Jesus

3 Mary was immersed in her own thoughts

4 Yehuda would have liked to believe in Jesus
   but found it impossible

5 Jesus answered Andrew and Philip, 'I am
   going to Capernaum. Follow me'

6 'Be silent, Satan', Jesus said, 'I command you
   unclean spirits from the pit of hell—leave him!'

7 The boy went into terrible convulsions and,
   after a rending paroxysm, he lay still

8 Peter stared at the newcomers with suspicion

9 Jesus got into the boat and sat in the prow

10 Simon Peter took Jesus up to his house where
   a great crowd followed and spilled over into
   the courtyard

11 Matthew, the tax-collector

12 Jesus went to sit near the door and told them
   the story of the prodigal son

13 Jesus went up to the dead child and knelt
   close beside her

14 'To doubt so much,' said Jesus to Thomas,
   'must mean that you long for certainty, and to
   know the absolute truth'

15 To the jealous resentment of Herodias, Herod
   openly lusted after Salome

16 Salome began to dance, at first slowly and then
   with increasing tempo and passion

17 'I swear', boasted Herod, 'that I will give her
   anything she asks'

18 'I want', she said, 'the head of John the
   Baptist'

19 Herod gave the order and John's end was swift

20 The burial of John's headless corpse
   completed, one of the Zealots said bitterly,
   'The Romans will never be left to rule at ease'

21 One of the Zealots threw a handful of sand on
   to the grave and the other mourners followed
   in turn. Judas Iscariot was the last to make the
   gesture

Very soon after he had emerged from his temptation experience, Jesus returned to Nazareth. Two women who saw him come into the town raced to tell Mary that he was back and that he had gone straight to the synagogue. So Mary prepared herself and also went down to the synagogue. It was the Sabbath and the congregation was just finishing the recital of the 18 Benedictions. The Rabbi had read from the Law and it was now time for the lesson from the Prophets. It was the custom for someone from the congregation to read the lesson from the Prophets, and the Rabbi looked round to see who could best be called. Before he had made up his mind, however, Jesus came forward and taking up the roll began to read. He read from the book of the prophet Isaiah:

> The spirit of the Lord is upon me
> because he has anointed me to bring good news to the poor.
> He has sent me to announce to the prisoners that they will be liberated
> and to the blind that they will see again;
> to send away in freedom those who have been broken by life;
> to announce that the year when the favour of God will be shown has come.

Jesus handed back the roll and said quietly, 'Today this passage of scripture has come true as you listened to it'. At first there was a shocked silence and then the congregation began to buzz with discontent. One cried out, 'Isn't it Joseph's son, the carpenter?' Another, 'How can he dare to make such a claim!' Yet a third, 'What do you mean? The prophecy you read can be fulfilled only by the Messiah, at the coming of the Kingdom of God.' There were murmurs of indignant agreement from the scandalized congregation. Jesus said, 'The Kingdom of God comes not in a way foreseen by men. The Kingdom of Heaven – behold – is suddenly amongst you. Repent and believe the good news.'

Andrew and Philip, two disciples of John who had followed Jesus to Nazareth, were in the congregation and in Jesus's claim they found the fulfilment of what John had said about him.

While some members of the congregation left the synagogue in high dudgeon, others remained still arguing. Jesus rose to his feet and Yehuda the Rabbi came over to him. Yehuda would have liked to believe in him but found it impossible. He was obviously sorry. Jesus put a hand on his arm and said, 'No prophet is accepted in his own country', and then, in a louder voice, to the entire congregation he said, 'Blessed is he who is not ashamed of me'.

The voices had now become threatening.

'What are we waiting for?'

'Rabbi, make him leave!'

'Liar!'

'Twister of the sacred scriptures!'

'How can he be the Messiah, dressed in rags like that?'

'He didn't say he was the Messiah.'

'What else could he mean?'

'Throw him out!'

The women were looking with disapproval at Mary and one said, 'Thank God your husband, didn't live to see this day'. But Mary was immersed in her own thoughts.

In the roadway outside the synagogue the men of the village had resolved to make an example of Jesus. 'Leave this to us, Rabbi,' said one voice, while another cried, 'Throw him over the cliff!' And so when Jesus appeared, in spite of the efforts of some to stop them, they began to hustle him to the cliff outside the town. When they came in sight of the cliff, however, the crowd seemed somehow less determined. Jesus offered no resistance whatever. He and the mob confronted each other. Quite suddenly and quite quietly, the crowd opened up in silence on either side to let him pass through, and Jesus walked serenely away.

As he was walking along the road, Andrew and Philip caught up with him. Andrew said, 'Master, we were sent by John the Prophet to make ourselves known to you. I am Andrew, a fisherman of Capernaum, and this is Philip.'

Jesus answered, 'I am going to Capernaum. Follow me'. And Philip said: 'Gladly'.

'Where is John?' Jesus asked.

'He has been arrested by King Herod Antipas', Philip answered.

As they walked through the fields, Philip said to Jesus, 'John said to us when he saw you "Behold the Lamb of God. It is Jesus, not me, that you must follow". He also said that anew his joy was fulfilled, and then the soldiers came and took him away.'

They were now in sight of Capernaum. Andrew said to Jesus, 'Anything that attracts crowds is dangerous these days. We saw that again in Nazareth, but,' he went on 'Capernaum should be a safer place to work from', and he pointed at the town across the lake.

Andrew said, 'It is a bigger town, for one thing. It is less narrow-minded, and I know from experience that the fishermen are ready for a change.' So they came to Capernaum which is a port and one of the largest towns surrounding the lake. It was a frontier town also, through which the road to Damascus and the far east passed. It was therefore an important commercial town, as well as an important fishing port.

Jesus was preaching to a lively congregation in a colonnade at Capernaum. Amongst the listeners there was a young man, John, the John who was one day to write a gospel. He was listening, and smiling sometimes in admiration of Jesus. Jesus said, 'I bring you the good news that you have all awaited. God today fulfils the promise he made to our people Israel, and reconciles himself to you. He reconciles himself to those who are near, and gives peace to those who are far away.' There was a stir among the listeners when Jesus went on, 'Whoever believes in this word will be freed by God from captivity, the captivity of sin. Sin has brought you no satisfaction. You have sold your souls for nothing. And freely God forgives you. He invites you to partake of his banquet. Come, every one of you, sinners and wretches, I proclaim to you the day of forgiveness.'

There upon, someone broke in, 'But surely the rewards will be greater for the righteous.

Surely people who have observed the Law all their lives will get better places at the banquet than sinners.'

Another man objected, 'Of course God is merciful and can forgive everything, but the sinner must show he is truly repentant and do penance. Do you now suggest that God wants nothing from us in exchange for his forgiveness? Is that right, or have I misunderstood?'

Jesus answered, 'The distance between man and God is vast. No human steps could ever cross it. Here then is the good news I bring to you. You don't have to cross it. God is coming to you to save you, all of you, even the most wretched. Do not shut the door in his face.'

In addition to preaching Jesus performed many striking and merciful acts in Capernaum.

A boy, demon-possessed, violently interrupted him by shouting, 'Leave us alone! What have we to do with you, Jesus of Nazareth? Are you come to torment us? To destroy us?' And the boy fell to the floor, writhing and foaming at the mouth. His father tried, without avail, to help him.

Jesus said to the father, 'How long has he been this way?'

The father answered, 'Since he was a child, and the demon often has thrown him into the fire and into water to destroy him. If you can do anything, have mercy and help us.'

Jesus answered, 'If I can? Everything is possible to him who believes.'

The man answered desperately, 'I believe. Help my poor faith.'

Jesus went over to the boy and addressed him with an imperious gesture. 'Be silent, Satan,' he said, 'I command you unclean spirits from the pit of hell – leave him!' The boy went into terrible convulsions and, after a rending paroxysm, he lay still, breathing deeply.

'Take him home,' said Jesus. 'Go in peace.'

This amazing miracle greatly disturbed the congregations. They talked about it to each other and related what had happened to newcomers just arriving.

One old Pharisee addressed Jesus, 'I suspect a danger in all this,' he said. 'Just because you have a certain power – and we admit that, for we saw it exercised just now – we cannot be expected to believe blindly in all that you say. This kind of power doesn't prove anything at all. For all we know it could have come from Satan.'

Jesus smiled at him. 'How can Satan cast out Satan?' he asked. 'If a kingdom is divided against itself, it is bound to collapse. Therefore, it is through God that I cast out devils, and I did it so that you might know that the Kingdom of God has come upon you.'

Jesus and his little group of disciples were walking by the lakeside. There were Andrew and Philip and young John. 'Everyone in our family,' said John, 'is a fisherman. Andrew knows us well. But I was sent off to get learning.'

'All you were fit for perhaps', said Andrew jestingly.

'And what did you learn?' Jesus asked.

John replied, 'That two and two make four – sometimes. That most people seem to be here to be knocked down. That getting on is a fine thing. That birth is the beginning of death.' John looked intensely at Jesus. 'I have learned,' he said, 'that there is only one Law. The Sadducees now proclaim only the written Law. The Pharisees proclaim the written Law plus all kinds of rules that tradition has added. We need clarity.'

Jesus put his hand on John's shoulder, and John said, 'Can I stay with you, Rabbi?'

Then they heard voices in the distance, and looking across the lake they saw the silhouettes of the returning fishing boats against a fiery sky. Andrew pointed them out 'There is my brother now, Simon Peter', and John added. 'And my brother James.'

Peter was shouting in anger as usual, and Andrew said, 'He doesn't really mean it. He is a good man, in spite of his loud mouth.' And Andrew shouted to the boat, 'What's the matter, brother – a poor catch?'

Peter looked up and saw the group on the shore. 'Bad? Bad and bad again. Nothing. Empty nets. Then when I get home the tax collector buzzes round me like a stinking horsefly. ''Where are your taxes?'' Well, let him go and catch them. Let him put some fish in the lake.'

Andrew was embarrassed by Peter's roughness, and decided to introduce Jesus to him in the hope that the introduction would take the edge off his anger. Andrew said, 'Peter, this is the man I told you about.'

The boat had reached the shore. Peter stared at the newcomers with suspicion. Jesus walked into the water and placed his hand on the boat, looking at Peter. He said, 'Don't stow your sails. Go out again. I will come with you.'

Peter objected, 'But we've just come in. Pull the boat up!' he ordered his crew.

Andrew went to the boat and implored Peter. 'Please,' he said 'do as Jesus tells you.'

Peter was about to give him a rough answer, but his rage was calming. He was curious to see what the newcomer, Jesus, could do. He looked at Jesus, who was staring out over the lake, indifferent to the dispute between the brothers. Jesus got into the boat and as it began cutting through the waves again, sat in the prow. He leant forward to gaze into the water in which he trailed his hand. Peter and Andrew sat near him. The other boat, carrying James and John, followed closely. Philip was in Peter's boat. Jesus continued leaning over the prow with his eye fixed on the water. Suddenly there was a ruffling of the surface, as if a slight breeze had blown upon it. Jesus cried, 'Now let down your nets!'

Peter made one last objection. 'What do you mean,' he said, 'I tell you there are no fish. I've been fishing for hours without result.' But he obeyed all the same, as did the others. The nets were lowered between the two boats and the ropes tightened. The fishermen shouted excitedly, 'Pull! Pull! Pull!' The nets were pulled to the surface, crammed with fish. Peter pulled with all his might. Although he was bent with the effort, he turned his face towards Jesus, 'Who are you? What are you?' he cried, amazed. Jesus answered, 'You must follow me, and I will make you fishers of men.'

When they regained the shore the lakeside was crowded with people. Other fishermen hurried over to discuss the record catch. Women and children came running to see the great sight of the overladen boats. Even Malachi and Naham, two Pharisees who worked as basket weavers, had left their work to see what was happening.

The town square of Capernaum was the wealthiest part of the town. There merchants offered their finest wares for sale, there money-changers set up their stalls, and there the tax-gatherers sat at the receipt of custom. Matthew, the tax-collector, having heard the remarkable story of the huge catch of fish, asked the man he had just relieved of dues – which the man described as a daylight swindle – exactly what had happened. The man was ready enough to talk. He had been there, he said, but could see little for the great crowd round the boats. That something very wonderful had happened, both at the colonnade where the boy was healed, and on the lake when the healer showed seasoned fishermen where to net a record catch, he had no doubt. No doubt whatever.

Simon Peter took Jesus and those who were in the boats up to his house. A great crowd followed, who pushed into the house and spilled over into the courtyard so that it was all but impossible to get to the door. Realizing the difficulty, a small group of men carrying a stretcher bearing a paralysed man, struggled to manoeuvre the stretcher up the outside staircase and on to the roof.

Inside, while Jesus was talking to the crowd, Peter's wife's mother was whispering excitedly to a friend. 'You know how I was. I couldn't stand up this morning, I was so sick and weak with the fever. But the moment Peter brought *him* in to see me I was made well, and now I feel fine. Marvellous! It's almost impossible to believe!'

At that point the raised voice of Naham broke into Jesus's preaching. 'Rabbi!' he cried. 'You say the Kingdom of Heaven is at hand, but when will it come?'

'When you see a cloud moving from the east,' Jesus answered 'you immediately say rain is coming, and so it happens. When the desert wind blows, you say it will be hot and so it is. If you can read the signs in the earth and the sky, how is it that you cannot read the signs of the times? The Kingdom of Heaven is here, now.'

As he finished a great commotion began to arise in the crowd. Its cause was soon apparent. Matthew the tax man and two bodyguards were pushing their way into the house.

Tax-collectors are seldom popular, but among the Jews they were the most despised and hated of men. For one thing, they worked for the detested Romans and were therefore regarded as traitors. And for another, over and above the amount of tax demanded by the Romans they were allowed to squeeze a profit for themselves, and were often remorseless in their exactions. Moreover, they had to collect taxes from the prostitutes, with whom, since there was no place for them in more respectable society, they tended to consort; hence the association of 'tax-gatherers and sinners'. In the eyes of decent people they were unclean. They were forbidden to enter the synagogue. They could not be called as witnesses in a lawsuit. They were even forbidden to enter any private house. If they did so they rendered the house unclean; and anyone entering the private house of a tax-gatherer rendered himself unclean.

When therefore Matthew arrived at Peter's house and actually pushed through the door, the impetuous Peter was thrown into a towering rage. 'Out of my house tax-gatherer!' he roared. 'We don't want the place defiled.'

Then Jesus, with a disarming smile, called out to Matthew, 'You seem to be unwelcome here. I don't know your name though I am aware of your occupation'.

'My name is Matthew or Levi', Matthew answered. 'I am known by both names.'

'And by a good many other names as well,' Peter muttered.

'I think,' Matthew continued, addressing Jesus but beginning to back through the door, 'that sooner or later we shall meet at my place of work.'

'Tell me, Matthew,' Jesus called out, 'is your house near?'

'Why do you ask?' demanded Matthew.

'Because', Jesus answered, 'I would like to eat supper with you tonight.'

'You would actually enter the house of a sinner – a sinner who is an enemy of the poor!' exclaimed Matthew.

'I enter any house where I am welcome', Jesus answered.

And the astonished Matthew, almost incoherent in his eagerness, called out that the Rabbi would be more than welcome at his house with any of his friends who cared to come with him, and that he would leave forthwith to arrange a feast.

Soon after Matthew's departure a further disturbance occurred. The friends of the paralytic, having manoeuvred him up the stairs and on to the roof, proceeded to break through a section of it and lowered him, on his litter, to the feet of Jesus.

It was not difficult to break through the roof of an ordinary house in Palestine. The roofs were flat, made up of a series of beams stretched from wall to wall, with the space between them filled up with compressed reeds, rushes and rubble. To gain entry from the roof, therefore, it was necessary only to remove the filling between two beams and the way was open.

Not surprisingly, Peter was far from pleased at seeing his roof broken up. 'What are you up to?' he cried. 'You are tearing my house to bits.'

'There was no other way to get him in', the men on the roof called down apologetically.

The poor paralytic, who had been frantically holding to the stretcher with his one good hand, was in a state of intense agitation, laughing and crying at the same time. 'I've been this way for twenty years', he wailed. 'It is a curse from God, a punishment for my sins and the sins of my parents.'

Jesus knelt over him. 'Your sins are forgiven', he said. And Jesus stood up and faced the people, among whom were two astonished and fearful Pharisees.

'Rabbi,' one of them cried 'you must not speak so. It is blasphemy. Who can forgive sins but God?'

Jesus turned to him. 'Tell me,' he said 'which is easier – to say your sins are forgiven you, or to say get up and walk?' The Pharisees were silent, and Jesus continued, 'In order to show you that the Son of Man has the power to forgive sins . . .' He turned to the paralytic and said, 'Arise, take up your bed and away you go home'.

The expectant crowd saw the man rise up, at first with difficulty, then with growing confidence, until he actually took up his bed and moved away through the astonished crowd, which opened to let him pass.

Matthew's house was bigger and grander than its neighbours, but it stood apart by itself, as though they shunned its company.

His kitchen staff were working their hardest to prepare for the enormous party Matthew had hastily organized. All the rascals, all the hard men and loose women, with the tax-gatherers who were his boon companions, had been asked; and were eager to attend since they were curious about the new preacher and his sensational deeds.

That Jesus actually proposed to go to Matthew's house greatly disturbed his followers.

'He doesn't seem to realize the shocking scandal it will cause', grumbled James, and he appealed to Peter to remonstrate with Jesus.

Peter said, 'I've told him as plainly as words can. What more can I do?'

James said, 'Tell him again'.

And Andrew observed gloomily, 'It will about finish him. No decent people will want to hear him preach if he goes ahead'.

When Jesus joined them Peter, who was the angriest of them all, shouted at him, 'Matthew is a blood-sucker, the enemy of all decent hard-working people. I hate him'.

Jesus said mildly, 'Why don't you come to the party, Peter, you've been invited'.

'Never!' shouted Peter. 'If you can stomach the stench and the company, you go into the sty and sup with the pigs. But leave me out.' So Peter stayed behind. He had been drinking heavily and was beside himself with anger.

A crowd, including the Head Rabbi and some Pharisees, had gathered at a discreet distance outside Matthew's house, to see whether Jesus really would have the temerity to go in. When he arrived a Pharisee called out, 'Master, it's a scandal for you to eat with those people. Don't you know who they are? Thieves, whores, usurers, a corrupt and godless crew if ever there was one.'

A second Pharisee took up the complaint. 'They deny themselves nothing', he shouted in passionate tones. 'All our lives we've struggled to observe the Law, however hard and demanding. We've made endless sacrifices to keep ourselves undefiled in the sight of God. But those people! – well, if you choose to sit down with such leprous outsiders upon your own head be it. You'll become an outcast, like them.'

Jesus answered quite calmly, 'It is not the healthy who need physicians, but those who are sick. I have not come to call the virtuous to repentance but the sinners, and I tell you they will enter the Kingdom of Heaven before you do.'

James made one last attempt to dissuade Jesus from entering. 'Listen, Master, if you go and eat with these people they will contaminate you. The whole town will abandon you.'

Jesus looked at him gravely and said, 'James, the heart of the Law is mercy', and with that he turned to go into Matthew's house.

Matthew, surrounded by his guests, was waiting for Jesus to arrive. He had invited all kinds of low-life characters, kept women, prostitutes, vagabonds of all kinds. As he crossed the threshold Jesus said 'Peace on this house!'

Matthew pushed forward one of his companions. 'This is James, my brother,' he said, 'he is in the same business as I am.'

Jesus stretched out his hand towards James, the son of Alphaeus, Matthew's younger brother, who raised his goblet to Jesus in a kind of salute. 'I drink to you,' he said, 'in the name of all of us here. For one reason or another we are not welcome in those places where you preach and perform these marvellous acts everyone is talking about. But we want to hear you speak, and if you can talk to us here we will listen.'

So Jesus went to sit near the door, where those outside as well as inside could hear. And he told them the story we call the story of the prodigal son.

'There was a man,' Jesus said to them, 'who had two sons. The younger of them said to his father, "Father, give me the share of your estate which is coming to me anyway".

And the father divided his whole estate between them. Soon after, the younger son turned the whole of his inheritance into ready money, and went off to a distant country. There he squandered his whole fortune in a career of debauchery. When he had run through everything he had, a severe famine fell on that land, and he was very nearly destitute. So he went and took service with a citizen of that country who sent him out to his farm to herd pigs. He longed to satisfy the pangs of his hunger with the carob pods which the pigs were eating, and no one gave him anything.

'When he came to his senses, he said to himself, "How many of my father's hired servants have more food than they can eat, and here am I, ready to die of starvation! I will start out, and go to my father, and I will say to him 'Father, I have sinned against God and against you. I am no longer fit to be regarded as your son. Take me back as one of your hired servants.'" So he set out, and went to his father. His father saw him coming a long way away, and he was heart-sorry for him. He came running, and threw his arms round his neck, and kissed him. The son said to him, "Father, I have sinned against God and against you. I am no longer fit to be regarded as your son." But his father said to the servants, "Quick! Bring out the best robe and dress him in it. Give him a ring to wear on his finger, and shoes for his feet. Bring the specially fattened calf and kill it. Let us eat and celebrate, for this son of mine was dead and has come to life again; he was lost and has been found." So they began to celebrate.

'His elder son was out on the farm. When he came near the house on his way home, he heard the sound of music and dancing. He called one of the servants, and asked what was going on. The servant said, "Your brother has arrived, and your father has had the specially fattened calf killed, because he got him back again safe and sound." He was furious and refused to go in. His father came and pleaded with him to come in. "I have worked like a slave for you for so many years," he said to his father, "and I never disobeyed any order you gave me, and to me you never gave so much as a kid to celebrate with my friends. But when this son of yours, who squandered your fortune with prostitutes, arrives, you have the specially fattened calf killed for him." "Son," his father said to him, "you are always with me. All that is mine is yours. But we had to celebrate and rejoice, because your brother was dead and has come to life again; he was lost and has been found."'

When Jesus had finished his story there was silence. Then Peter, who had eventually followed the others to Matthew's house and had listened to the parable standing outside but close to the door, burst in and fell at Jesus's feet. 'I am not worthy to follow you Lord', he said in deeply emotional tones, 'I am a sinner.'

Jesus raised him up and said, 'Don't be afraid, Peter. Come, join us at the feast'.

High in the hills, in the castle of Macaronte Herod Antipas was considering arrangements for his birthday celebrations. He could faintly hear the noise of demonstrators outside who were shouting for the release of John the Baptist. John had dared publicly to rebuke Herod Antipas for seducing and then marrying his own brother's wife, Herodias, until finally, worn down by the nagging of Herodias, Herod had at last consented to arrest John, and he was imprisoned in the vaults.

'Let him go!' the demonstrators shouted. 'Tyrant, Adulterer, set him free!' Angry and not a little frightened, Herod gave orders for the demonstrators to be dispersed, and at the sight of advancing soldiers they scattered and fled.

Distraught by the interruption, Herod decided to go down and visit John. It was not the first time he had done so, and at each visit his respect for the Baptist increased.

John, more emaciated than ever, lay chained to a corner of the rough-hewn rocky cave which was his prison. Herod, unaware that Herodias, having crept after him down the stairs, was listening intently outside the cell, greeted John almost deferentially.

'What do you want of me?' he asked. 'I have to put up with endless insults from you and your followers. My father would have given you short shrift, I can tell you. What *will* satisfy you? You denounce my irregular marriage. Well, I begin to repent of that myself and have a mind to send Herodias back to her husband.'

The listening Herodias was profoundly disturbed and when Herod went on to say, almost plaintively, that it was no satisfaction to him to keep John rotting down there in the dark, and asked what John would do if he were released, she seethed with anger.

'My mission is over', John answered. 'I was but a forerunner, preparing the way for one who is greater than a prophet. He has appeared, and if I were set free, I should join his followers.'

Herod emerged from John's cell more uneasy than ever, and Herodias had no difficulty about getting away unnoticed.

Late that evening, when they were talking together, Herod told Herodias that as an act of clemency to mark his birthday, he was thinking of releasing John. It would be a popular gesture, pleasing to the mob. Herodias taunted him with being afraid of John, and when he angrily denied it she alternately nagged him and wheedled him until he agreed not to act in a hurry. He would continue to hold him . . . for the present.

Salome was Herodias's seductive young daughter by her previous marriage, and Herod, to the jealous resentment of Herodias, openly lusted after the girl.

Herodias looked at him in a calculating way. 'Very well', she said. 'Salome shall dance for you.'

Jesus and his small band of disciples had left Capernaum, and were bivouacking in the open fields. Jesus was sleeping quietly by a dying fire. Philip, James, and John's brother Andrew, were watching over him, while John was stretched out, also fast asleep. Matthew, the former tax-collector, who had not yet quite overcome his fear of being repulsed, was seated a little way apart, watching Peter who, beyond the hearing of the disciples, was engaged in a vigorous argument with his wife and mother-in-law. After some final emphatic observations by the latter the two women went away, the first looking resigned, the other plainly angry.

Peter came over and seated himself beside Matthew. 'Women!' he said disgustedly. 'Why don't they listen. I told my wife. I said, I shan't be away for long. The fishing is hopeless at this time of the year, anyway. I said to her, I'll come back in the spring.'

'Don't lie to yourself as well as her', Matthew said.

'Lie?' said Peter with a hint of truculence.

'Yes', said Matthew. 'You know it well. You'll never go back.'

'I certainly will', said Peter.

'No you won't', said Matthew. 'Never. You won't fish again. And you won't drink to excess again either. You'll never settle down in Capernaum now. None of us will. We shall never be the same again. Neither will the world. The event the prophets foretold, and for which the ages have looked, has come to pass. And we are the first to realize it.'

The next day Jesus and his disciples, to escape the crowds, had gone out on the lake in two boats, one of which was Peter's. When Jesus was ready to return they approached the shore. People saw them coming, and an expectant crowd again gathered at the lakeside. When the boats were moored Jesus, followed by Philip and Andrew, James and John, jumped ashore. Matthew hesitated a moment, and then he too followed. Peter, who had been testing the moorings, was the last to join the little group. Jesus began speaking to the crowd. 'Anyone', he said, 'who has left his house, or brothers or sisters, or father or mother, or wife or children, or land, for my sake, shall be rewarded a hundred fold in the life to come. Do not think,' he continued, 'I have come to bring peace on earth. I have not come to bring peace, but a sword. I have come to sow discord between a man and his father, between a daughter and her mother. A man's enemies shall be those of his own household. Anyone who prefers his father or mother to me is not worthy of me. He who finds his life shall lose it! He who loses his life for my sake shall find it!'

At that point a man rushed up to the crowd clamouring to be taken to Jesus. The crowd tried to silence him, but Jesus, aware of the urgency in the man's tones, ordered him to be brought forward and the man, having been pushed up to Jesus, prostrated himself.

Jesus raised him up, and the man at once burst out, 'My name is Jairus. I am an elder in the Capernaum synagogue. My little daughter is lying at the point of death. I beg you, come and lay hands on her that she may recover and live.'

'Take me to her', Jesus said, and Jairus hurried him away, followed by the disciples.

Friends and neighbours had gathered round the house of sickness, and with the arrival of Jesus were quickly joined by others. As Jairus was making a way through these bystanders a friend came from the house and gently detained him. 'Jairus,' he said, 'your daughter is dead. It is useless to trouble the Master further.' But Jesus said, 'Don't be afraid, Jairus. Keep on trusting', and he entered the house, where a great tumult of weeping and wailing was being made.

Jesus raised his hand to still the noise of mourning. 'Be quiet,' he said, 'the child is not dead, but in a deep sleep.'

Thomas, a servant of the house, was indignant at what he took to be callous showmanship. 'Who are you,' he demanded of Jesus, 'that you come here mocking our grief? You haven't even seen the poor girl. We have been anxiously watching her for hours and we *know* that she's dead.'

Jairus signed to Thomas to be quiet and sent the other people away. Then Jesus entered the sick-room. He went up to the dead child and knelt so close beside her that his breath almost stirred her hair. He spoke to her, whispering softly in her ear, 'Rise little girl, wake up'. The girl opened her eyes, turned toward Jesus, smiled at him, and scrambled from the bed. Taking her by the hand Jesus led her over to her parents, who by this time were on their knees. 'Give her something to eat', he said. 'Perhaps we could all do with something to eat', he added. As they led her away there was a noise of astonished rejoicing. People flocked round the girl embracing and caressing her.

The manservant Thomas, utterly confounded, wiped the sweat from his forehead, and
100

began apologizing to Jesus. 'Master,' he said, 'I'm, sorry for my rudeness. I thought the child was dead. No!' he cried defiantly 'she *was* dead. I saw it with my own eyes.'

Jesus smiled at him. 'Do you believe only what you see with your eyes?' he asked.

'I hardly know what to believe any more', Thomas answered. 'I find it difficult to credit what my eyes *have* seen today. I almost doubt the evidence of my own senses.'

'To doubt so much,' said Jesus, 'must mean that you long for certainty, and to know the absolute truth.'

'I do', said Thomas, 'I want to be sure.'

'Then,' said Jesus, 'follow me.'

'You mean, give up my work?' asked Thomas.

'Yes,' said Jesus, 'I want you.' And turning to Jairus he said, 'Jairus, will you give me your servant Thomas to be one of my disciples?'

'Gladly, Master, and bless his good fortune', said Jairus.

'Then,' said Jesus, 'Thomas must decide. Have you doubts about following me?'

'No', said Thomas after a long pause. 'I don't believe I have.'

While Jesus, amid scenes of growing enthusiasm, was moving from place to place around the lakeside, John continued fettered in his cell. One notable day Philip and Andrew, two of his followers, having bribed his guards, were admitted to see him. It was a very brief interview, held while the guards watched anxiously outside the cell.

Philip at once began telling John about Jesus. 'In front of huge crowds,' he said, in subdued, urgent tones, 'he drives out evil spirits, heals the sick and has even recalled the dead to life. He charged us with a message for you. "Tell John," he said, "that the lame walk, lepers are cleansed, the deaf hear and the dead are raised to life. Good news is proclaimed to the poor, and happy is the man who does not lose faith in me".'

'God be praised!' John exclaimed. 'My work is done. I bore witness that he was the one, and now I know that my witness was true. The doubts that have sometimes visited me, lying inactive in this dark place, have been answered. Tell all my disciples to follow him, and proclaim with him the Kingdom of Heaven.'

In the banqueting hall of his castle-palace Herod, who had been drinking heavily, was entertaining a large company of guests – nobles of his court, Roman officers, and the most distinguished citizens of Galilee – to a birthday feast. Once, during a temporary lull in the festive babel, a voice seemed to echo hollowly from somewhere below, 'Woe unto them that call evil good and good evil, and are wise in their own eyes. Woe unto them...' But the guests started talking loudly again to cover their embarrassment, and Herodias gestured to the musicians to strike up. She leant over and said something to Salome, who grimaced and went over to Herod and kissed him playfully on the ear.

Herod gazed at her with sensual approval and called out in loud slurred tones, 'Come! You must dance for us, my dear. We've been promised something new and specially exciting. Don't keep us all waiting. Dance!'

The company applauded loudly. Herodias again gestured to the players and the music changed, becoming dark, sensual, intense. Salome began to dance, at first slowly and then with increasing tempo and passion. Herodias watched carefully to see Herod's reaction to her daughter's inflammatory performance. When the dance ended Salome moved over to the royal couch. The guests applauded wildly, and someone called out to

101

Salome, 'What shall the princess ask the king?' Salome, still panting from the dance, lolled beside Herod. 'I swear', Herod shouted boastingly, 'that I will give her anything she asks, even half my kingdom.'

Salome went back to her mother, and after a whispered consultation returned to Herod. 'I want', she said, 'the head of John the Baptist.'

The drunken Herod, sobered by abrupt fear, stared at her in disbelief. 'It is impossible,' he said, 'you can't mean it. Ask for something else.'

'You swore', Herodias reminded him. 'You swore before all your guests. Shall it be said that King Herod does not keep his promises?'

Herod glared at her with malignant hatred, but gave the order. A soldier was despatched and John's end was swift. In the shortest possible time a servant, followed by two guards, entered the banqueting hall bearing a salver covered by stained cloth. Herod stared balefully and there was a sudden silence. Bowing low the servant placed the tray before Salome. Herodias left her place and walked fascinated towards it. 'That is your gift', she said to Salome, and with a swift gesture she uncovered the tray.

Some of his followers, having secured the headless corpse of John the Baptist, were burying it in the open country which had for so long been John's home. A number of Zealots had infiltrated the group, to the resentment of his more intimate followers; and one of the Zealots had brought with him a friend, Judas Iscariot.

The burial completed, one of the Zealots said bitterly, 'The Romans will never be left to rule at ease. At present we strike in the dark, but the day will come when God will send us a leader, and then we shall strike openly.'

'You mean real war?' Judas queried. 'The people of Israel against the Roman Empire?' – and everyone stared at him.

'Jesus of Nazareth', the Zealot said. 'Do you know him?'

'I have heard him preach, many times', Judas answered.

'Is he the man to fix our hopes on?' asked another Zealot.

'Ah! I cannot answer your question', said Judas. He gestured towards the grave, '*He* might have done so. I know what he said to two of his disciples who managed to see him in prison. He said "I bear witness that he is the one. Tell all my disciples to follow him, and proclaim in his name the Kingdom of Heaven".'

'We know all this', said another of the Zealots impatiently, 'but is he the one?'

Judas thought for a moment. 'I have seen him many times', he said. 'He has power. Startling power. He could give the right lead to the whole nation. But give him time. Let him fulfil the present phase of his mission first. He is drawing the crowds. People swarm after him with ever-growing enthusiasm. But he may need . . . guidance. If he will have me, I intend to become one of his disciples.'

'Well then,' said one of the Zealots, 'will you keep in touch with us?'

'If you wish', said Judas.

Then one of the Zealots turned toward the grave and said, 'Peace be on you, John. Your blood cries out for vengeance, but may your soul find rest in the company of the righteous'.

He threw a handful of sand on to the grave, and the other mourners followed in turn. Judas was the last to make the gesture.

6

9

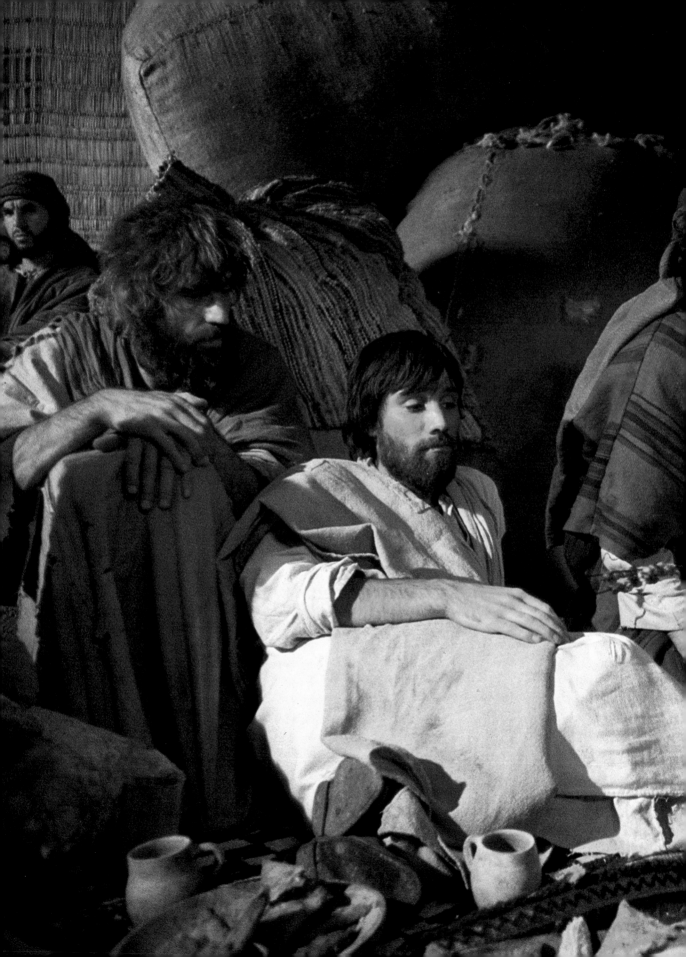

21

PART 4

THE TWELVE ARE
SENT OUT

PHOTOGRAPHS

As a prostitute, Mary of Magdala suffered a good deal of scorn and verbal abuse, particularly from her women neighbours, and was sometimes a prey to attacks of a more dangerous nature. Taking a cue from their elders, the boys of the small town not only called after her but sometimes kindled fires close to her door, threatening the very house itself. More than once Mary was compelled to extinguish the flames with a heavy blanket, and then to trample out the embers. It was not in her nature to submit meekly to these attacks. On one occasion she had just managed to quench a particularly dangerous fire when one of the bigger boys crept forward and whispered, 'Can't I come inside for a few minutes?' 'Come closer,' she murmured, 'and I'll tell you what we'll do.'

The boy advanced more confidently, and Mary, seizing him by the hair, gave him several resounding cuffs. 'Now get out, you little swine, before I really lose my temper!' she shrieked. The boy ran off laughing and shouting, 'She's mad', and his companions took up the cry in a taunting chant.

Her neighbours complained bitterly to one another of the disturbance, laying all the blame, as was to be expected, at Mary's charred door. Before she arrived, life in the neighbourhood was peaceful and quiet. Now it was becoming quite intolerable.

But Mary was hard to dislodge. Added to her fighting spirit was the fact that she had money. Plenty of it.

That night a merchant named Elihu, one of her regular patrons, was preparing to depart when he said casually, 'By the way, there was a friend of yours in town today'.

'I have no friends', said Mary coldly, for she was feeling tired and dispirited. 'Oh yes you have!' said Elihu mockingly, 'though you may not know him. It's Jesus, this new prophet everyone is talking about. He's the friend of all the outcasts and sinners, and takes it upon himself to forgive them for everything – all their sins. The lot.'

'Have you seen him?' Mary asked curiously.

'Seen him! If you have to go round on business as I have,' said Elihu, 'you can't help seeing him. You just turn a corner or go into a tavern and there he is. He's been going round for over a year now. Have you never come across him?'

'You forget,' said Mary, 'that I sleep for most of the day.'

'True,' said Elihu, 'I quite forgot that. Well, great crowds gather to hear him preach wherever he goes. He has remarkable powers of healing too. Yet he thinks nothing of eating and drinking with thieves and whores.'

Mary looked at him incredulously and handed him his cloak.

'It's strange goings-on for a prophet,' Elihu said musingly. 'He's actually called a tax-gatherer to join the band of disciples who go round with him. Says it's not the righteous but the sinners who need help. So you see, after all you have a friend, whatever the neighbours say.'

With an exclamation of impatience Mary took the money he held out to her and showed him to the door.

'Same time next week?' Elihu asked briskly, but Mary shut the door without answering. She went to the bed, and flinging herself on her back stared at the ceiling. She was wondering what kind of preacher it could be who had a good word to say for sinners.

The next day found her among a crowd of people making for the open country outside Capernaum. The sun was shining and everyone seemed in a good-humoured holiday mood. Coming up to a family group, a husband, a wife, one child walking and another in arms, she smiled at them. But the smile died away from her lips at the response. The man recognized her and hurried his family away.

After that her steps became laggard. She fell behind the crowd which, some way ahead, was leaving the road and beginning to cross a large open field. Feeling lonely and discouraged she was thinking of turning back when a girl hurried by, anxiously balancing a mug of water. She saw the girl holding the mug to an old woman who had sunk to rest by the side of the road, obviously ill and exhausted. As she came up with them the girl called out excitedly, 'Jesus is coming along the road by the lake. If we cut across the field we will be able to see him. Help me with her, would you? She's ill, and if we don't hurry . . .'

The old woman muttered endlessly to herself, 'Just to touch him . . . just to touch his clothes even . . . I know I'll be all right then . . . I know it will put me right.'

Mary looked at the girl and then looked at the old woman. 'Well', she said, 'if you think it will do any good.' She stooped and put the old woman's arm round her neck. The girl and Mary between them started to help the old woman towards the field.

'You shouldn't have brought her,' Mary said, 'she's very ill.'

'That's exactly why I did bring her', the girl said.

The crowds were surrounding Jesus. Mary and the girl with the sick woman had almost to fight their way through. 'She'll be crushed,' said Mary, 'I told you this is not the place for a sick woman.'

From the shouting it was clear that Jesus was near, but Mary had had enough of the pushing and shoving. 'I'm getting out', she said.

The girl looked anxiously at the old woman. 'If I could only get near him', said the old woman. 'He would not even have to stop and speak to me. If I could only touch his clothes I'm sure I would be cured.'

'All right', said the girl, and looked hopefully at Mary for her continued help.

'No,' said Mary, 'you must go on without me. I've seen enough. I'm going home', and she turned away.

Jesus stood in a little space the disciples had cleared for him amid the crowd, but the crowd kept pressing in. Suddenly Jesus twisted round. 'Who touched me?' he asked. The people were silent, perplexed by his question.

Peter, in his usual impulsive way, said, 'Master, you are hemmed in by all these people, and yet you ask who touched you?' – as if to say 'Don't be silly, you can't avoid being touched.'

'Someone touched me,' insisted Jesus, 'I felt strength going out of me.' At this the crowd parted a little and the old woman came forward.

140

'Sir,' she said, 'I thought it would make me better just to touch the hem of your robe as you went by. Forgive me, I have been ill for 12 long years.'

Jesus helped her to her feet. 'Daughter, go in peace. Your faith has made you well again.'

Later that same day as Jesus and his disciples were walking along the road by the lakeside, still attended by an enthusiastic crowd, they were stopped by a young man, very richly dressed, who rushed up to them. 'Good Master', the young man began. Jesus broke in, 'Why do you call me good? No one is good but God.'

'Tell me, Master,' said the young man, 'what must I do to have eternal life?'

'You know the commandments', Jesus said. 'You must not kill; you must not commit adultery; you must not steal; you must not bear false witness; honour your father and your mother.'

'I have kept these commandments all my life', said the young man.

Jesus stopped and looked the young man fully in the eyes. 'What is the first commandment?' he said. 'You must have no other God but me', the young man answered.

'Yes,' said Jesus, 'you must love the Lord with all your heart. Go sell all that you have and give it to the poor, and you shall have treasure in heaven. Then come and follow me.'

The young man was obviously shocked. 'Sell everything?' he said, 'Everything I own? Everything my father slaved for?'

Jesus answered, 'You cannot serve two masters, God and money'.

Sadly he walked slowly away. Jesus turned and spoke to the others. 'How difficult it is,' he said, 'for the rich to enter the Kingdom of Heaven. Truly, it is easier for a camel to go through the eye of a needle than for a rich man to enter the Kingdom of God.'

The disciples were astonished. Judas called out from the crowd, 'Master, we all own something. Who can be saved?'

'Don't be afraid', Jesus answered. 'With God's help, all things are possible.'

As Jesus once more stopped to preach, a group of richly-dressed elders joined the crowd, amongst them Simon the Pharisee, and Joseph of Arimathea, who had come all the way from Jerusalem to hear him. Jesus was standing in the shade of an olive tree, and his sermon went like this:

'No one can be a slave to two owners,
for he will either hate the one and love the other,
or he will be devoted to one and despise the other.
You cannot be the servant both of the God of heaven
and of the god of this world's wealth.

'That is why I tell you,
Stop worrying about what you are going to eat and drink
to keep you alive;
stop worrying about the clothes you are going to wear
to keep your body warm.
Surely there is more to life than food,
and more to the body than clothes?

'Look at the birds of the sky.
  See how they do not sow or reap
  or collect things into storehouses.
And yet your heavenly Father gives them their food.
Are you not much more valuable than they?'

Judas Iscariot, who was standing next to Simon, nudged his elbow and said 'Look over there, that's Joseph of Arimathea from Jerusalem'. But Simon said impatiently, 'Be quiet and listen'.

'Can any of you add half a yard to his height
  by worrying about it?' Jesus continued,
  'And why worry about clothes?
Learn a lesson from the way in which the wild lilies grow.
They do not toil or spin.
  But I tell you,
that not even Solomon in all his splendour
was robed like one of these.
You have so little faith.
  If God clothes like that the wild flowers
  which have one brief day,
and which tomorrow are used to make a fire to heat an oven,
  can you not depend on him far more
  to clothe you?
So then, make up your mind to stop worrying,
  and to stop saying,
  "What are we going to eat?"
  or, "What are we going to drink?"
or, "What are we going to wear?"
  These are the kind of things
  which the people who don't know God keep thinking about.
Your heavenly Father knows you need all these things.
  Make the Kingdom of God,
  and life in loyalty to him,
the object of all your endeavour,
  and you will get all these other things as well.
  So then, make up your mind to stop worrying about tomorrow.
Tomorrow will worry about itself.
The day's trouble is quite enough for the day.'

As Simon the Pharisee listened, he turned to Joseph of Arimathea and said, 'It seems to me unwise to speak like this to ignorant people'.

'I heard nothing', said Joseph of Arimathea, 'that has not already been said by the prophets.'

'You may be right,' said Simon, 'but I should like to question him further about his doctrine.'

142

'Why not invite him to an evening meal at your house?' suggested Joseph.

'If you think he would come', said Simon who, as a very wealthy and superior person, thought Jesus might be embarrassed in the company of his social superiors.

'With a mind like his,' said Joseph, answering Simon's look and tone of voice, 'he would certainly not be afraid to come, nor afraid of discussing his ideas with anyone.'

A little later, as Jesus and his disciples were resting, Judas came up to Jesus and said, 'Master, I would like to become your disciple'.

'What is your trade, my friend?' asked Jesus.

'Well, I have never carved wood, or beaten copper, or caught fish, as most of your men seem to have done', said Judas. 'My father was a prosperous builder who said "My son must be worthy of his patrimony. He shall never have calloused hands or have to brush brickdust from his hair. Instead my money shall go to making him into a scholar!" So behold the scholar! A scholar who finds much useful employment. I read and write Hebrew, Greek and Latin, I translate documents, and this has become a country of many tongues. May a scholar serve you? I am ready to be baptized in order to be washed free of the past and forgiven.'

'If you repent,' said Jesus, 'your Father in heaven has already forgiven you.'

The disciples offered round broiled fish spread on loaves of bread. They did not care for Judas's self-assurance nor did they like his superior social status. 'Do you need a man like me?' persisted Judas.

Jesus stared at him. 'The tree is known by its fruits', he said. 'Come, stay with us.'

Late in the afternoon Mary Magdalene was sitting by the roadside, tired and dispirited again. One of her sandals had broken and she was trying to mend it. She had still a long way to go before she reached home. Then along the road came the old woman and the girl whom she had helped in the morning. The old woman recognized Mary and they came over to see her.

'Look!' said the girl, 'she is better.'

'I just touched the hem of his robe,' the old woman said, joyously, 'and I was cured.' But Mary was too depressed to share the good fortune of other people. 'I'm grateful to you too, my dear,' the old woman continued, 'for without your help, we could not have got near. What is your name? Have you got far to go?'

'My name is Mary,' Mary answered, 'and I come from Magdala.'

'That's a long way from here and you're tired,' the old woman said. 'Why not come home with us for the night?'

Mary was touched by the old woman's invitation, but knowing it would not have been given had her trade been known, and feeling self-conscious, insecure and shy, she refused brusquely. 'No,' she said, 'I had better go home.' The old woman laid her hand on Mary's shoulder and then turned and went on her way with the girl.

Mary continued to sit by the roadside. A small company of people passed, and one of the men slackened his pace and leered back at her, knowing who she was. She got up angrily, and hurled several stones after him. As the man hastily rejoined his group she turned and hurried after the old woman and the girl, calling to them as she went. They looked back and stopped when they heard her voice.

'Did he really cure you?' she asked as she caught them up.

'Yes indeed', the old woman answered. 'Blessed be the womb that bore him!'

On Mary's face a look of hope began to dawn. This Jesus who healed the sick and said he had come to help sinners – there must be something in him.

Another day and yet another huge crowd had gathered to hear Jesus preach. Many social classes were represented in the crowd, for Jesus was arousing an ever-widening interest throughout the entire nation. Pharisees, dedicated to the meticulous observance of the law, were present in considerable numbers. Sadducees, those wealthy aristocrats who were ready to collaborate with any government which would guarantee them the continued enjoyment of their privileges, were also present, although in lesser numbers since they resided almost exclusively in Jerusalem. Zealots, those fanatical nationalists who would use any means to sweep the hated Romans from Palestine, were present in strength, moving purposefully among the crowd.

Philip was standing with Andrew, watching the huge crowd building up. 'Do you see those two?' he inquired, indicating two fiercely scowling men who were pushing forward. 'They're Zealots.'

'So I see', Andrew answered. 'Interest in Jesus seems to be growing daily more intense. The Sanhedrin have sent observers all the way from Jerusalem.'

'Does it remind you of anything?' Philip asked.

'It reminds me,' said Andrew, 'of John the Baptist, and the way interested groups tried to use him just before the end.'

The huge crowd took some time to arrange itself, and by the time Jesus had finished speaking it was late afternoon. People who had been hanging on his words were suddenly aware of being hot and tired and very hungry.

'Master,' John said urgently 'we must send all these people away. We have nothing to give them, and they need food. They should set out at once for the villages where they can get something. Even then . . .'

'We must not send them away empty', said Jesus. 'You give them something.'

There was an awkward silence. 'How', asked Philip, 'can we possibly give them something to eat? There are thousands of them.'

'What food have you?' asked Jesus.

'Well here are five barley loaves and a couple of fishes', said Andrew.

'Good!' said Jesus. And having blessed the loaves and fishes he said, 'Start distributing them among the people'.

The disciples were taken aback, for at a rough estimate they reckoned there were five thousand people present.

'Some of the people have luncheon baskets', Jesus continued. 'Borrow them. Put one loaf or one fish into each basket, and carry them round for the people to help themselves. When everyone has had enough bring back what is left.'

The disciples were too astonished to obey. They just stood staring, until Peter cried out, 'Go on! Do what he says.' Then they put the few loaves and even fewer fishes into baskets and started going round. People reached into the baskets, took enough to satisfy their hunger, and the disciples moved on. The disciples' tramp through the crowd

144

went on and on, and the people took and took, but no matter how much they took the baskets never emptied. The disciples were bewildered, amazed. The crowd realized more slowly the staggering happening of which they were a part. When they did so an excited clamour arose. It grew and grew as more and more people gave expression to their amazement and joy. Then the disciples began gathering up the leftovers, and they filled twelve baskets. These they brought to Jesus. At this sight the enthusiasm of the people broke all bounds. They were shouting, crying, laughing, embracing one another.

At the peak of the uproar a young man jumped on to a rock and addressed the crowd.

'Remember the words of the prophet Jeremiah', he cried. ' "The days are at hand when I will raise a tree of virtue for David – one who will reign as a true king, shining in wisdom, sowing honesty and righteousness through Israel." Here is your king – of David's blood, wise and righteous, a worker of miracles. Is it not this man the Lord has sent to be a ruler of Israel? The one who must cast out the heathen and the servants of the heathen? Who will bring to an end the rule of Rome and the puppet of Rome in Galilee? Jesus of Nazareth is the Messiah promised by God!' There was a roar of acclamation from the crowd and the wildest excitement prevailed.

Some of the Zealots, among them Amos and Simon, stood watching with Judas. The Zealots were infected by the surging enthusiasm of the crowd. 'God be praised' said Amos, 'this is the man promised by the scriptures. Take me to him.'

But as the others grew more heated Judas became cooler. He was beginning to mistrust the Zealots. 'We must not act hastily', he said. 'We should first get together and examine every aspect of the situation very thoroughly . . .'

They met the next day in a room in Simon's house. The atmosphere was tense with dark passionate feelings. 'Without the slightest doubt,' said Daniel the Zealot, 'God has sent us the leader in Jesus. He can, he must take us to victory over the oppressors.'

'Death to the tyrant Herod!' growled Joel.

'What are we waiting for?' Hosias demanded. 'John prophesied that the Kingdom of God is at hand. But the Kingdom must have a visible leader – a Moses, a Joshua, a conquering hero like David. We know Jesus has the authority and the power. It is time to proclaim him openly as the God-appointed King the people will follow.'

'March on Jerusalem', exulted Daniel. 'Gather an army and at Passover establish the Kingdom of Heaven on Earth.'

'Wait!' said Judas commandingly. He had been listening with growing impatience to the fiery talk, and his attitude to the Zealots was now one of scornful opposition. 'This is a time for clear thinking, not the ridiculous fantasies in which you are indulging. You want to kill Herod and march on Jerusalem? You could have your skulls crushed for saying that, and some day they will be. It would bring death and destruction on all of us if Jesus were manipulated by explosive people like you. His words will speak louder than your blustering eloquence, and as for his enemies – what will defeat his enemies? What will disarm them? Your madness or his mission?'

'It's our duty to proclaim him', said Daniel stubbornly.

'His deeds proclaim him already', said Judas.

'But we must keep him in his mission', said Hosias. 'Construct around him a great united party from the multitudes who are flocking out to hear him, young and old, rich and poor, all classes and all ages. Today the party. Tomorrow the nation.'

'Take us to meet him, Judas', urged Joel. 'We must talk to him.'

'No', said Judas. 'The Baptist was right, men must change before kingdoms can fall.'

'Don't stand in our way, Judas', Daniel said threateningly, 'I'm advising you.'

Amos, the fanatical Zealot leader, now intervened with a great show of coolness and common sense to lower the rising temperature of the meeting. 'Judas can't stop us, brothers', he said. 'We mustn't get heated. But he's far too valuable an ally to lose. I like many of his ideas. Oh, Herod must die; that's quite certain. He must pay in blood for the blood of the Baptist. But I agree with Judas. Jesus should be kept out of the picture – for the time being. It will be safer not to approach him at present, wait until the Passover in Jerusalem, that is the time for you to bring him to us Judas. We have our own brothers in the Temple Guard. We shall arrest the Sadducees and order them to proclaim Jesus King of the Jews. If they refuse – well they can join their Roman patrons in a blood bath. But they won't refuse. Not when they see we have the power as well as the will. Do you agree?'

His fellow conspirators were deeply impressed. They argued with enthusiasm, all except Simon who for some time had been changing his mind about the cause and had become more and more disillusioned as he listened to their fanatical plans.

'No, Amos,' he said, 'I don't agree.'

They looked at him, startled, shocked.

'I have listened carefully to each of you in turn, and, sadly, not one seems to grasp what the coming of Jesus signifies. Like you, I believed that the people of Israel would rise at the coming of the Messiah and break their chains. But I have become convinced that the mission of Jesus means something far greater than the overthrow of our enemies by armed might. Through him Israel will be reborn, not by outward force but by a change within. Men must themselves change before the world is changed, the rebirth must come in our hearts.'

There was a moment's silence, then Amos said pleadingly, 'But Simon, you can't give up the cause like this. We've believed in it, prayed for it, worked for it, all our lives.'

'Brothers,' said Simon, 'I haven't given up the cause – not God's cause. But revenge breeds revenge. Kill and you will yourselves be killed . . .'

'Either you are with us or against us', Amos interrupted harshly. 'You must choose.'

'I have already chosen', said Simon. 'I shall follow Jesus of Nazareth if he will accept me.'

'He will accept you', said Judas, and having said their farewells, he and Simon left together.

The evening of the same day Jesus, responding to the invitation of Simon the Pharisee, was sharing a meal in Simon's house. Joseph of Arimathea was present along with several Pharisees of Capernaum. The guests had witnessed the feeding of the five thousand, and their attitude to Jesus was one of respect tinged with awe. No one quite knew what to say until Jesus put down his cup and, smiling a little said, 'John the Baptist came neither eating bread nor drinking wine, and many of you said he was possessed by devils. I come eating and drinking freely with you and you will say this man is a glutton and a drunkard, a friend of tax-collectors and sinners!'

146

'Rabbi,' Simon answered, 'you do us an injustice. We respect your achievements. We understand their importance. But we are anxious to know what will happen next? Do you want to change the Law? We hear that you chose to heal sick people on the Sabbath when you could easily have waited until the next day. Do you not want our people to respect the Sabbath?'

Jesus remained silent for a few minutes and then said, 'If one of you had a sheep, and it fell into a pit on the Sabbath day, would you not go and get it out? God made the Sabbath for man and not man for the Sabbath.' 'We understand that,' said Simon, 'but simple people need clear simple precepts. Is there not a danger of confusing ordinary people?'

'Without the Law what will happen to us?' asked a Pharisee.

'The Law has held Israel together for more than a thousand years', said Joseph of Arimathea. 'Without the Law, can Israel survive?'

'Do you really believe', said Jesus, 'that to observe the Law is enough? What is the heart of the Law?'

Joseph of Arimathea answered, 'You must love the Lord your God with all your heart, with all your soul and with all your strength. This is the greatest of all the commandments.' And they all gravely agreed.

Jesus answered, 'You have said well. You are not far from the Kingdom of God, Joseph of Arimathea. But there is another commandment no less great. "You must love your neighbour as yourself".'

'But who is my neighbour?' asked Simon.

By way of answer Jesus told them a story to which they listened with deepening interest. 'There was a man,' he said, 'who was on his way down from Jerusalem to Jericho, when he fell into the hands of brigands. They stripped him naked, and beat him up, and went away and left him more dead than alive. It so happened that a priest was coming down the road. When the priest saw him, he passed by on the opposite side of the road. In the same way, a Levite arrived at the spot. He went and looked at the man, and then passed by on the opposite side of the road. A Samaritan who was on the road, came to where the man was lying. He was heart-sorry when he saw the state the man was in. He went up to him, and poured oil and wine on his wounds, and bandaged them. Then he put the man on his beast, and took him to an inn, where he looked after him throughout the night. Next morning he took out two silver coins and gave them to the inn-keeper. "Look after him," he said, "and, if you incur any additional expense, I'll square it up with you on my way back." Which of these three would you say was a neighbour to the man who fell into the hands of the brigands?'

There was a silence while the guests thought over what Jesus had said. Suddenly the silence was shattered by a loud commotion. Mary of Magdala was struggling determinedly with the servants to be allowed to enter the house. 'I will come in!' she shouted. 'Don't think you can stop me.' She pushed one of the servants aside, burst into the room where Simon was entertaining his guests, and rushed over and fell at Jesus's feet weeping. While everyone watched in outraged astonishment she wiped Jesus's feet with her hair, kissed them and began to anoint them with precious ointment from an alabaster jar.

Simon said icily to Mary, 'This is no place for you, woman. Leave quietly and at once', while he whispered to a friend, 'If this man was really a prophet he would know what kind of woman this is.'

'Simon', said Jesus.

'Yes', Simon answered, returning his attention to Jesus.

Jesus turned to the woman. 'You see this woman?' he said to Simon. 'When I came into your house, you did not give me any water to wash the dust off my feet. This woman has drenched my feet with her tears, and has wiped them with her hair. You did not give me a kiss of welcome. But since she came in she has not stopped kissing my feet. You did not anoint my head with oil. She has anointed my feet with perfume. This is why I tell you that, although she has sinned greatly, her sins are forgiven, because she loved greatly. He who is forgiven little, loves little.' Jesus passed his hand over Mary's beautiful hair. 'Daughter,' he said, 'your sins are forgiven you.'

The other Pharisees were embarrassed, but Joseph of Arimathea was watching Jesus with renewed interest and respect. 'Your faith has saved you', Jesus said to Mary. 'Go and sin no more', and he helped Mary to her feet. Her face, now filled with love and hope, was transformed. She turned to go. Jesus picked up her jar of ointment and held it out to her. 'Daughter,' he said, 'take this ointment and keep it for my burial. Go in peace.' Amid a profound silence Mary took the ointment and went.

When their training was sufficiently advanced, the day came when Jesus sent out twelve of his inner band of disciples as 'apostles' or messengers. He sent them two by two for mutual support. The names of the twelve apostles were Simon Peter and his brother Andrew; James, the son of Zebedee, and John his brother; Thomas and Matthew, the tax-gatherer; Philip and Bartholomew; James, the son of Alphaeus, and Thaddeus; Simon, the Zealot, and Judas Iscariot.

Before they left Jesus gave them instructions for the mission. He said, 'Cure the sick, raise the dead to life, cleanse the lepers, eject the demons. Do not lay in a stock of gold or silver or copper coins in your money-belts. Do not take a beggar's knapsack for the road, nor two shirts, nor shoes, nor a staff. Whenever you enter a town or village, look for someone who deserves the presence of my messengers, and stay there until you leave it. When you go into a house, give your greeting to it. If anyone refuses you a welcome or a hearing, as you leave that house or town, shake the last speck of its dust from your feet, as if you were leaving a heathen town. I am sending you out like sheep among wolves. You must therefore show yourselves to be as wise as serpents and as pure as doves. Do not worry about how you are to speak, or about what you are going to say. What you are to say will be given you at that time, for it is not you who are the speakers; the speaker is the Spirit of your Father, speaking in and through you. Freely you have received, freely give.'

Thus charged they went here and there to towns and villages throughout Galilee, being sometimes welcomed and sometimes turned away. Once Peter, supported by Thomas, was preaching to a small crowd in a village square, when a young man shouted at him, 'Jesus of Nazareth is an impostor and you are impostors too. You are all impostors.' Peter would have felled the youth with a blow, but Thomas restrained him. Whereupon Peter threw a muscular arm around the youth's neck and put a hand over his mouth, thus immobilizing him, though the young man continued to struggle. Then Peter kissed him on the head. 'I ask your pardon, my dear son,' he said, 'but truly, you must keep your big mouth shut. Listen, all of you, my brothers', he cried, releasing the discomfited youth. 'The Kingdom of God is at hand. The day of the forgiveness of sins is upon us. A day of love and patience and forbearance.'

John preached in a village close to Nazareth, where many of the villagers who heard him had been to Nazareth and had seen or heard Jesus. Some of them regretted their one-time hostility to Jesus. John said, 'Do not think that Jesus, who was your close neighbour, who was born of your own people, do not think that Jesus has come to destroy the Law and the prophets. He has come not to destroy, but to fulfil. Whoever hears his words and believes in him has eternal life. And his word is that the hour is coming and now is when the dead will hear the voice of the Son of God, and they that hear shall live. Marvel not at this, for the hour is coming when all who are in the grave shall hear his voice, and shall come forth – they that have done good unto the resurrection of life, and they that have done evil unto the resurrection of judgement.'

When he had finished preaching, John went to visit Mary, Jesus's mother. He knelt before her. 'You are his mother', he said. 'Blessed are you among women.' Mary laid her hand on his head with affection. 'Anyone', she said, 'who obeys our Father in heaven is his brother, sister and mother.'

In a certain city while the disciples were present, an attempt was made on Herod's life. He was being carried through the streets, lolling back contemptuously on the silken cushions of his litter, when Joel the Zealot rushed out from the crowd with a knife in his hand. Joel's eyes were wild for he was in ecstasy. 'Kill the tyrant!' he cried, slashing at Herod through the curtains of the litter. Herod's robe was slit and his arm gashed. 'Help!' he cried, 'help me!' A guard struck down Joel. Amos, Daniel and other Zealots rushed from the crowd screaming, 'Kill him, kill the tyrant!' But by this time the guards were ready. The Zealots were cut down or were dragged away as prisoners.

While Herod's wound was later being dressed he complained bitterly of the outrage. 'I could have been killed', he moaned. 'The guards were far too slow. You know why this happened? Two disciples of Jesus of Nazareth have been preaching in the town creating disaffection, stirring up trouble.'

'Your Majesty', answered the chief of the guard, 'Jesus has no interest in the Zealots.'

'How do you know?' retorted Herod. 'Who told you?'

'One of his disciples, a very intelligent and honest man', the chief of the guards answered.

'Rebels still make use of him just the same', said Herod.

'They made use of John the Baptist,' said the chief of the palace guard, 'and, Your Majesty, with respect, John the Baptist has been more dangerous since his death than he was when he was alive.'

Herod well knew this. 'Then don't just stand there,' he said testily, 'tell me what to do.'

The chief of the guard suggested that Jesus should be driven from Galilee, and all the roads except the road to Judea should be closed. 'Let the Imperial Procurator worry about him', he suggested. But Herod clutched at another idea.

'If he is a prophet,' he said, 'perhaps I should meet him. I should have him perform a miracle – here – in this very room.'

'It might be dangerous,' the chief of the palace guard answered, 'his miracles have a strange effect on people, sometimes changing their entire outlook on life. Does Your Majesty wish to risk such a change?'

'No,' said Herod, 'I want to be safe. Drive him out. And have no mercy on these Zealots. Dispatch them at once.'

The surviving Zealots were dragged from their cells and with their wrists bound above their heads they were tied to a rough wall of planks. At the word of command a line of soldiers hurled javelins at them, and within a short time they were dead.

Simon and Judas were on their way to meet Jesus and the other disciples. Simon received news of the death of the Zealots. He was deeply moved.

'Were they all killed?' asked Judas, 'All of them?'

'All of them', said Simon. 'They were my brothers. I lived with them since I was a boy.'

Judas put his hand on Simon's shoulder to comfort him. 'I know they were mad,' said Simon, 'I know, but they meant well, how devoted they were! They thought they could force God's hand.'

'You warned them what would happen', said Judas. 'Poor Amos. To die like that.'

'How good and strong he really was', said Simon.

'Don't grieve', urged Judas. 'Jesus will go to Jerusalem and meet with the Sanhedrin and arrange for action on the plane that his mission demands – with no bloodbath. Come on', said Judas, 'Let's find the Master.'

The apostles were gathered with Jesus after a frugal meal. Jesus by this time knew that the culmination of his mission was drawing near, and he knew what that culmination would be. So he said to the disciples, 'And who do the people in Galilee say that I am?'

Bartholomew answered, 'Some say, John the Baptist. They won't believe that he is dead.'

'Some know that he is dead, but they think that you are John the Baptist come back to life', said Andrew. 'Others say you are Elijah back from the grave.' (It was believed that Elijah would return as the forerunner of the Messiah, when the Messiah was about to appear.)

'Others say Jeremiah or Ezekiel', added Philip. It was the belief that Jeremiah, before Jerusalem was devastated, took the Ark of the Covenant and the Altar of Incense, and hid them in a secret cleft in Mount Nebo, and that he would return to bring them out before the Messiah was due.

Then Jesus said, 'And who do you say that I am?'

Judas was ready to give the right answer at once but he left it to Peter to speak, and while the rest hesitated Peter came in strongly, 'I say you are the Christ, the Son of the Living God.'

Jesus answered, 'You are indeed blessed, Simon Barjona, for it was no human being who revealed this to you; it was my Father who is in heaven. I tell you, you are Peter – the man whose name means a rock – and on this rock I will erect my Church, and the powers of death will be helpless to harm it. I will give you the keys of the Kingdom of Heaven, and whatever you forbid on earth will be forbidden in heaven, and whatever you allow on earth will be allowed in heaven. To you all I say this: that Peter has spoken the truth, and now you know what it is. But you must not reveal it to any man. The time is not yet come for that. It will come, for the time is here for me to go to Jerusalem.'

Simon the Zealot looked doubtfully at Jesus, but Judas was cheerful at the prospect of going to Jerusalem.

'Yes, Master,' he said, 'you must go to Jerusalem. The whole city awaits you. The Elders of Israel must know and recognize you.'

Jesus looked very keenly into Judas's eyes. 'No, Judas,' he said, 'in Jerusalem the Son of Man will be rejected by the Elders and the Chief Priests of the Temple, and unbelievers will scourge him, mock him, murder him. Then after three days he will rise again.' The disciples looked at him in horror.

There came a day when Jesus delivered his most famous sermon to the disciples and others who had gathered around him. We call it the Sermon on the Mount. Jesus said:

'O the bliss of those who realize
    the destitution of their own lives,
for the blessings of the Kingdom of Heaven
    are theirs here and now.
O the bliss of those whose sorrow is sore,
    for they shall find courage and comfort.
O the bliss of those who strength is in their gentleness,
    for they shall enter into possession of the earth.
O the bliss of those who hunger and thirst
    for all that sets them right with God,
    for they shall be satisfied to the full.
O the bliss of those who treat others with mercy,
    for they shall be treated with mercy.

O the bliss of those who are pure in heart,
    for they shall see God.
O the bliss of those who make men friends with each other,
    for they shall be ranked as the sons of God.
O the bliss of those who are persecuted
    for their loyalty to God's way of life,
for the blessings of the Kingdom of Heaven
    are theirs here and now.
Yours is this bliss,
when men shall heap their insults on you,
    and persecute you,
      and tell every wicked kind of lie about you for my sake.
When that happens,
rejoice and exult in it,
for you will receive a rich reward in heaven,
for it was thus that they persecuted
    the prophets who lived before you.'

'Just so, your light must shine
    for everyone to see, so that,
when they see the lovely things you do,
    it may make them want to praise
    your Father who is in heaven.

'But I tell you
    not to resist evil, but,
        if anyone slaps you on the right cheek,
        let him slap you on the other as well;
If anyone asks you for anything,
    give it to him,
and do not refuse anyone
    who wishes to borrow from you.
'You must be perfect as
    your heavenly Father is perfect.

'Don't make a habit of judging others,
    if you do not want to be judged yourselves.
For the verdict which you pass on others
    will be the verdict that is passed on you.
You will get in exactly the same proportion
    as you give.'

John said: 'How can we, imperfect as we are . . . ?' Jesus said:
    'Keep on asking, and you will get;
    keep on seeking, and you will find;
    keep on knocking, and the door will be opened for you.
    For everyone who keeps on asking gets what he asks for;
    he who keeps on seeking, finds;
    if a man keeps on knocking, the door will be opened.
    Is any of you likely to give his son a stone,
        if he asks for a loaf?
    Is he likely to give him a snake,
        if he asks for a fish?
    If then, evil and ungenerous as you are,
        you know how to give your children good gifts,
    how much more can you depend on your Father in heaven,
        to give good things to those who ask him for them?'

At the same time Jesus taught his disciples a prayer, which we still call the Lord's Prayer.
    'So, when you pray, pray like this:

Our Father in heaven,
May your name be held in reverence,
    May your Kingdom come,

May your will be done,
    as in heaven, so on earth.
Give us today our bread for the coming day.
Forgive us for our failures in our duty to you,
    as we have forgiven those who have failed
    in their duty to us.
Do not submit us to any time of testing,
    but rescue us from the Evil One.'

Into the Sermon on the Mount Jesus put the very essence of his teaching.

That very night Jesus was sitting quietly looking into a small fire, still awake. All the disciples were asleep, except Peter. Peter approached Jesus. 'Master', he said.

'Yes?' said Jesus.

'You said', Peter reminded him, 'that you are going to Jerusalem and that in Jerusalem they will kill you.'

'Yes', said Jesus.

'If that is true,' Peter said, 'it is our duty to keep you from going. We must not allow it to happen.'

'Peter,' Jesus rebuked him, 'you are thinking as men think, not as God thinks. The devil is speaking through you.' Then he stood up and said to Peter, 'Get behind me, Satan'.

Shortly afterwards Jesus and his men set out on the fateful last journey to Jerusalem. Jesus's face was set and determined as he moved at the head of his little band along the road, but his followers, remembering his warning of what awaited him there, were apprehensive and downcast. James and John were at the rear of the party.

'One more halt,' James said, 'and we shall be nearly there.'

'And Jerusalem will be swarming with pilgrims up for the Passover', John answered. 'What will he say to them now, I wonder? And will he go straight into the city and start preaching?'

James shook his head. He had no idea what was going to happen. 'He prophesied that he will suffer death there', he said.

And Peter, who overheard him, interjected, 'Then let us go, that we may die with him'.

As the group moved on, Jesus striding purposefully in front, the others lagging a little way behind, a man on horseback came riding swiftly toward them from the direction of Jerusalem. Reaching the travellers he dismounted, and having made eager inquiry of the disciples, hurried up to Jesus.

'Master,' he said, 'Martha and Mary, the sisters of your friend Lazarus in Bethany, have sent me to find you. Lazarus is dying.'

'My poor friends!' said Jesus. 'I will go to them. Return and tell them I shall be coming.'

'We must mend our pace if we are to be there in time', said Peter, who with the other disciples had gathered round during the conversation.

'No Peter', said Jesus. 'There is no pressing hurry. We shall arrive in three days' time. This illness will not end in death, but will reveal the glory of God; and through it the Son of Man will be glorified.'

In due time Jesus and his men reached the street in Bethany where Lazarus lived.

Martha, who must have been on the watch, ran out to meet them. She was clearly deeply distressed. When she reached him, Jesus took her by the hand. 'It is too late, Lord', she said. 'If only you had been here my brother would not have died.'

'Your brother', said Jesus, 'will rise again.'

'I know that he will rise at the last day', said Martha.

Then Jesus said, 'I am the resurrection and the life. In death to believe in me is to live again. In life, for any man, to believe in me is never to die. Do you believe this?'

Martha answered, 'Yes, I believe that you are the Christ, the Son of God, he who was to come into the world'.

'Where have you laid him?' Jesus asked.

'Come and see', said Martha.

So they came to the village burial place. The tomb of Lazarus was in a cave, with a stone placed across the opening. Jesus, with Martha and the disciples, stood before the tomb. Mary was there with some other mourners, and Mary was weeping. When she saw Jesus, she knelt at his feet. 'Lord,' she said, 'I prayed and prayed for you to arrive. You would have kept Lazarus from dying.'

Jesus raised Mary to her feet and put his arm around her. He came near to the tomb. He was deeply moved. Jesus wept.

'See how he loved him', said one of the bystanders.

'He opened the eyes of a blind man', said a second. 'Could he not have prevented this man's death?'

'Take away the stone', Jesus said. Some men started to obey when Mary broke in, 'He has been dead for four days. His body must already be decaying'.

'Did I not tell you', said Jesus, 'that if you believed you would see the glory of God?'

The stone was now removed. People were expecting the stench of decay. It did not come. Jesus fell into deep prayer. Then he lifted up his eyes to heaven. 'Father,' he said, 'I thank you for hearing my prayer. I knew indeed that you always hear me, but I speak for the sake of all those who stand round me, so that they may believe that it was you who sent me.' The entrance to the tomb was dark. There was a long pause and all eyes were fixed on the opening in the rock.

Jesus stood up and called in a loud voice, 'Lazarus, come out!' There was a deep silence. Suddenly there was a glimpse of something white stirring in the gloom of the cave. The patch of white grew gradually larger. Lazarus, his body and limbs swathed in grave clothes and his head bandaged, appeared in the entrance to the tomb. He moved slowly out of the darkness into the light. 'Loose him', said Jesus, 'and let him go.'

Martha and Mary, trembling, went to their brother and began by uncovering his face. Lazarus opened his eyes. His face was that of one who has been beyond death and is then summoned back to life, and after a moment his eyes came to rest on Jesus.

Jesus said, 'I am the resurrection and the life. In death to believe in me is to live again. In life, for any man, to believe in me is never to die'.

The incident was awesome to those who witnessed it. Everyone was overwhelmed. And it was to have a marked effect on the reception Jesus was to receive in Jerusalem.

6

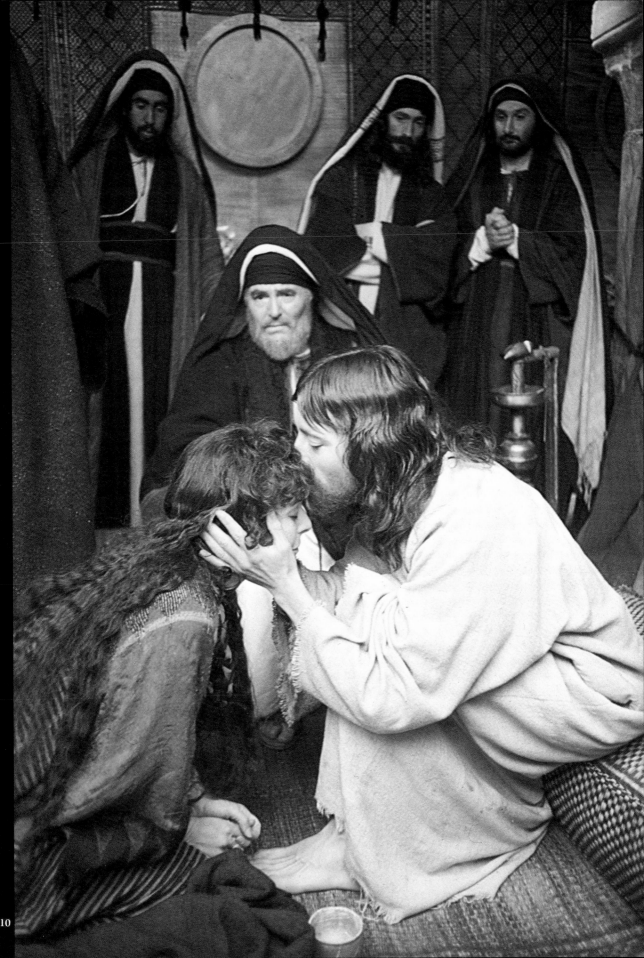

19

PART 5

THE ROAD TO CALVARY

PHOTOGRAPHS

Zerah was young, a much respected intellectual, and very ambitious. A member of the Sadducees, he was also a priest of the Temple, and it was through him that Judas made contact with the Establishment. He and Zerah met first in one of the Temple rooms.

'I am extremely flattered', said Zerah, 'that you have asked to see me. Why did you pick me out, by the way?'

'There are many in Israel who think your influence in the Sanhedrin affords great hope for the future', replied Judas. 'Since the matter I wish to lay before the High Priest is of the utmost importance for the future of Israel, as well as of immediate urgency, I could think of no better approach to His Highness than through you. You have a reputation for adroitness in practical affairs in addition to your great reputation as a scholar. With respect, you get things done.'

'Since you know so much about me,' said Zerah smoothly, 'you won't be surprised to learn that I know a good deal about you. And of course we all know a great deal about your Rabbi from Nazareth – miracles of healing – production of vast quantities of food out of thin air – raising the dead – extraordinary! – To put it mildly. But is there not just a chance that his astonishing powers come not from the highest but the lowest possible source: in short, from Satan? How can we be sure? I wish my duties had left me time to see your Jesus for myself.'

'I wish they had', said Judas. 'You would then need no persuading that he is the only man who can bring peace to Israel.'

'Oh?' said Zerah sharply.

'The Zealots started to realize it,' said Judas, 'and so, you might be surprised to learn, did your own Temple Guards. As for the Romans – they are eminently practical. They would welcome anyone who could pacify the country. And if it were to cost them nothing, so much the better. The Sanhedrin should recognize Jesus as the true Messiah and say to the Romans . . .'

'What', Zerah broke in, 'should we say: "Look Caesar, we have a new ruler – one from the Royal House of David. One in whom we have every confidence, who preaches peace, tolerance and love, even to you Romans. Therefore you may calmly withdraw your troops. We no longer need them . . ."'. Judas chose to ignore the irony in Zerah's words.

Zerah looked at him thoughtfully. 'Let us be serious', he said. 'Judas – is that your name? – you can be a very worthy friend to the Elders of Israel. And they will, I am sure, show their gratitude when the time comes. You said something about the Temple Guards. What did you mean?'

'Like you,' said Judas, 'I have my sources of information. I am not exactly eager to reveal them.'

'All right,' said Zerah, 'you and I should not quarrel. What do you want me to do?'

There was silence for a moment. Then Judas spoke very deliberately. 'Let Jesus of Nazareth prove himself before the elders of Israel', he said.

'I think', said Zerah, 'I can promise you that he will have that opportunity. Meanwhile I shall learn more about him.'

Jesus was about to enter Jerusalem through the Damascus Gate. A vast and highly excited crowd swarmed about the roadway. Judas pushed his way through the jabbering, gesticulating throng, and as he did so he overheard snatches of conversation.

'A great prophet.'

'Greater even than John the Baptist, some say.'

'They say he can raise the dead.'

'They say nonsense then. Nobody can raise the dead.'

'Except God. He can do all things.'

'And didn't he empower Elisha to raise the son of the Shunamite woman from the dead?'

'Glory in the highest! Nothing can resist the power of God's anointed.'

'A new King of the Jews. One who will overthrow our oppressors and rule in equity.'

In their joyful excitement they strewed the roadway with palm leaves and flowers. As he at last came into view a roar of welcome went up, exciting them to still wilder frenzies of enthusiasm.

'Hosanna! Blessed is he that comes in the name of the Lord!'

But there were some to whom his appearance, instead of being a stimulus, acted as a check to enthusiasm. A strange entry this for the rumoured leader who was to overthrow Rome! An emaciated man, riding an ass, preceded by eleven rather ragged supporters.

'Is *this* the new king?', one asked.

'Riding on a donkey!', said another derisively.

But a loud confident voice answered the sneer, 'Zechariah foretold it, "Jerusalem, daughter of Zion, behold thy King cometh unto thee, humble and meek, riding on an ass".'

The acclamations became louder, more joyful than ever as the crowd moved slowly beside and before Jesus, waving their palm leaves, even casting their garments on the roadway for the new king to ride over.

'Hosanna! Blessed is he that comes in the name of the Lord!'

The uproar startled a small group of Sadducees proceeding along a nearby street. They stopped a man who was hurrying past and asked what it meant. 'The prophet, Jesus of Nazareth', the man said excitedly, 'he is here!'

They let the man go. One of them said, 'There is no great cause for concern', but they turned and walked after the man toward the source of the disturbance, all the same.

Conveniently stationed at a high window Zerah looked down on the slow-moving procession. He was surprised by the appearance of Jesus, but was more interested in the appearance of Judas, whom he could see, curiously foreshortened, smiling with satisfaction at the way things were going.

When the group of Sadducees arrived on the scene they could not help but be impressed by the enthusiasm of the crowd. Pushing their way to the front they emerged close to

188

Judas. On every side the people were waving, laughing, shouting, 'Blessed be the king that comes in the name of the Lord! Glory in the highest'. One of the Sadducees tried to address the crowd, but realizing the futility of public protest turned angrily to his companions. He had to shout to make himself heard above the acclamations. 'This is sheer fanaticism. Such cries are dangerous. They must be stopped.'

Jesus, as the ass moved slowly forward, overheard the protest. 'If *they* held their peace the very stones would cry out', he said.

White with anger the Sadducee again turned to his companions. 'Did you ever hear such arrogance?', he cried. 'How dare an upstart Galilean speak thus to a member of the Sanhedrin?'

Progress through the thronging crowd became a snail's crawl, but at length Jesus and the disciples reached the entrance to the Temple, when Jesus dismounted and two of the disciples led away the patient ass. Jesus mounted a few of the Temple steps, and signalled that he wished to speak. His voice rang out.

'The time has come for the Son of Man to be glorified. I tell you, and it is true, if a grain of corn does not fall into the ground and die, it remains alone. But if it dies, it produces a large crop.' The silence of the crowd deepened. Jesus went on, 'It is only for a little while longer that the light is to be with you. Get on your way while you have the light so that darkness may not come down upon you. When a man walks in the dark, he cannot see where he is going. While you have the light, believe in the light, that you may become sons of light.' Then, as if communing with himself, he added, 'I am in distress of soul just now. What am I to say? Am I to say: "Father save me from this hour?" But no! It is for this purpose that I have come to this hour. Father, glorify your name.' A voice came from heaven, 'I have glorified it already, and I will glorify it again'.

The crowd began shouting again, 'God bless the Son of David. Praise God in the highest heaven. God bless the King of Israel!'

Zerah, who had descended from his observation post as the procession moved on, had made his way to the Court of the Priests by the time it reached the Temple steps. He was discussing the uproar with a small group of priests from among those appointed for the day, who looked to him for a lead. Some of them urged him to intervene at once.

'Intervene?' said Zerah. 'No. At least, not yet. I must confess that I am fascinated by the power of this man over the people. We must try to find out where his power comes from.'

'He is certainly capable of the most astonishing manifestations of power', said Eliphaz.
'He raised one of his friends from the tomb.'

'A clever trick before coming to Jerusalem', said Jonah.

'You still can't deny that . . .' began Eliphaz, but Zerah broke in, stopping the argument before it developed. 'Please be advised. Don't act impetuously.' Then he called Eliphaz aside for a private word. 'Eliphaz,' he said, 'would you ask the Captain of the Temple Guard to report to my Lord Caiaphas – immediately.'

Just then, there came a loud outburst from somewhere within the Temple, and the priests hurried out to see what was happening. In the Court of the Gentiles they saw Jesus overturning the tables of the money-changers and driving their owners away. 'It is written,' he said, 'my house is a house of prayer. But you have turned it into a den of thieves.' And after he had finished with the money-changers, he began to drive out the sellers of oxen, sheep and doves for the sacrifices.

To understand his violent reaction to the money-changers we must remember that Gentiles were not allowed to proceed beyond the first court, which had become something like an eastern market place. The Temple tax, to which everyone was liable, had to be paid either in Galilean shekels or in shekels of the treasury, since, unlike other coins, these shekels bore no portrait of a ruler. Such portraits were reckoned among the graven images explicitly forbidden by the Law of Moses. Hence while Tyrenian, Phoenician, Egyptian, Greek and Roman coins would serve for ordinary transactions, they had to be changed into the acceptable shekels to pay the Temple tax. It cost the pilgrim a coin called a *ma'ah* to get his money changed, a *ma'ah* being the equivalent of a new penny. If changing the money involved getting change, the pilgrim had to pay the money-changers another penny for the service. That is to say, he had to pay two new pence (or $1\frac{1}{2}$ cents), one to change the money and one to get his change.

As for the sellers of livestock for the sacrifices, what happened was this. You could buy your doves outside the Temple, but they had to pass the scrutiny of inspectors appointed by the Temple authorities. Any animal offered for sacrifice had to be without spot or blemish, and the Temple inspectors were quite certain to find some blemish or some flaw in victims purchased outside. They would thus say to the person seeking an animal to sacrifice, 'You would do best to buy your animal from our stalls, for there they have already been inspected'. This seems harmless enough until it is realized that there were times when a pair of doves cost as little as 5 new pence outside the Temple and as much as 75 new pence inside it. Jesus's wrath was therefore aroused for two reasons. The stalls where the sacrificial victims were sold turned the Temple Court into a market place. What should have been a place of prayer had become a place of noisy bargaining. Secondly, as we have seen, the poor pilgrims were the victims of a swindling racket, and Jesus was unwilling to see any man exploited.

Inevitably, the sensational and spectacular action of Jesus created trouble. The merchants were astonished, afraid and resentful. The priests were shocked. Zerah made an attempt to be conciliatory. He went up to Jesus. 'Rabbi,' he said, 'I am Zerah, a priest of this holy place, and like my brethren, I have followed your mission with interest. We heard good things about you and we were glad. But what you have done here now shocks and surprises us. Do you want to destroy the sacred Temple?'

'The Temple is not mere stone', answered Jesus. 'It is the house of God. It cannot be destroyed so long as God lives there', and as he said it he placed a hand over his own heart. 'Destroy this temple,' he said, 'and in three days I will make it rise again!'

'It took centuries to build this temple. Do you think you can rebuild it in three days?', Zerah demanded.

'You have said it,' answered Jesus, 'but you have not understood.'

'Rabbi,' said Zerah threateningly, 'I understand better than you think. The Lord Caiaphas will be profoundly interested in all this.' And he went away.

Judas came up to Jesus. 'Master,' he said, 'that Sadducee is one of the most open-minded members of the Sanhedrin. He had every intention of approaching you in a friendly way. He wanted to understand your mission. Was it wise to discourage him?'

190

Jesus looked at him for a moment in silence, and then in a voice that held both sorrow and pleading said, 'Judas, open your heart, not your mind. Open your heart.'

Jesus was later to preach in the Temple portico, when his hearers included a sprinkling of Sadducees, Pharisees and Zealots, including Barabbas. Despite the opposition of the disciples, some enthusiastic admirers of Jesus brought forward a group of young children, who sang in a far from perfect chorus 'Hosanna to the Son of David'. The Sadducees and Pharisees were incensed by the use of the title.

'You deceive the very children', Samuel the Sadducee said contemptuously. 'Have you no shame?'

'Have you never read in the psalms', said Jesus '"Out of the mouths of babes and sucklings thou hast perfected praise"?'

Eliphaz, unable to stand any more, confronted Jesus truculently. 'By what authority do you do these things?', he demanded.

'Before I answer,' Jesus said, 'I will ask *you* a question. From where did John the Baptist receive the authority to baptize, from heaven or from men?'

Samuel the Sadducee began to say, 'From men,' but Eliphaz stopped him before he could get the words out. 'You fool!' he whispered. 'Do you want the people to tear you to pieces!'

'So,' said Jesus, 'John's authority was not from men. Then if it was from heaven, why did you not believe him? Answer me.'

There was a silence and then Eliphaz shouted furiously, 'We don't know. We can't tell.'

'John the Baptist,' said Jesus, 'came to you in the way of righteousness, and you did not believe him. Yet there were many sinners who believed. But you, even when you saw that they believed, you did not repent!'

'He who believes in me,' said Jesus, 'believes in him who sent me.' The priests and the Pharisees, scowling with anger, went away. Meanwhile Jesus, surrounded by some of his disciples and some of the people who had been listening to him, went towards the Portico of the Ablutions. Barabbas followed with some of his fellow conspirators. They passed two Temple Guards, friends of the Zealots, who kept watch, making sure they were not interrupted. Other people slipped away at the sight of Barabbas who, with only two of his followers, came up to Jesus.

'Master,' he said in low tones, 'I am Barabbas the Zealot. Amos sent us word about you before his murder. The Temple Guards are ready and so are my brothers. We will follow your orders to the end.'

Jesus raised his eyes to Barabbas, 'You have heard that it was said "You shall love your neighbour and hate your enemy." But I say to you, Barabbas, love your enemies and pray for those who mis-use and persecute you. The day of forgiveness is upon us.'

'Forgive Herod?' demanded Barabbas incredulously. 'Forgive the Romans?'

Jesus answered simply, 'You must change your hearts'.

Barabbas could not believe his ears. 'The Romans', he said, 'have killed dozens who were not even involved in politics. You can't mean to forgive that, Master. We must meet the sword with the sword.'

'All that take to the sword', said Jesus, 'shall perish by the sword. The new Jerusalem will not be created by armed might, uprising and murder. The wisdom of God will fill the land as water fills the sea. Barabbas, don't lose your confidence in God. His justice will come down among men, and the lion will lie down with the lamb. There will be no more hurting or destroying, and the voice of weeping *shall* be heard no more.'

Barabbas and the Zealots were plainly shocked and obviously bitterly disappointed. Jesus stood very close to Barabbas. He addressed him now with a more affectionate voice. He deeply wanted Barabbas to understand. 'I must', said Jesus, 'take on my shoulders the sins of the world. He who would follow me must do the same. The scriptures say, thou shalt not kill. But I say to you, anyone who is angry with his brother without a cause is guilty, and anyone who calls his brother a fool shall be in danger of hell fire.'

Barabbas and his Zealots stared at Jesus as if he was mad. They were incapable of understanding him. Judas's face was troubled. Jesus seemed to have rejected him as well as the Zealots.

The disciples came up to Jesus to tell him that a man was waiting in the hope of seeing him in the Court of the Gentiles, beyond which a Gentile could not come. Jesus went to meet him and found a Roman centurion waiting. The encounter caught the interest of the Roman guards in the Antonia Fortress, who were intrigued to see a centurion respectfully greeting Jesus.

'Lord,' said the centurion, 'I would like to ask you a great favour. I have a servant in my house who is very dear to me, more like a son than a servant. He is very sick, dying I fear. Lord, in all humility I ask. . . .'

Jesus broke in, '. . . that I should come to your house? Very well, I will come'.

'No, Lord,' he said, 'I am unworthy that you should enter under my roof. I know that if you say the word my servant will be healed. I am a man who knows all about discipline and authority. I myself have authority over 100 soldiers, and if I say to one "Do this", I know that he will do it. If I say to another "Go there", I know that he will go. I need not see, I know. So it is enough that you give the word, and it will be done.'

Jesus was deeply moved. He turned to those present and pointed at the centurion. 'Did you hear this man?', he said. 'I say to you all, I have not found faith like this among many in Israel.' Then his gaze, moving over the crowd, fell on the faces of the Pharisees and the Zealots, and they were grim. He laid a friendly hand on the centurion's shoulder. 'Go home,' he said 'your faith has cured your servant.' The centurion was astonished, not only at the promised miracle, but also that a Jew should voluntarily have touched a Gentile. Barabbas and his Zealots were standing a short way off. For them, that Jesus should have reached out in friendship to touch a Roman soldier was the last straw.

At that moment a very excited crowd entered the courtyard. The Sadducees Ezra, Jonah and Samuel held a terrified young woman in custody. 'No, no,' shouted the young woman, 'let me go!', and on all hands voices were raised. 'Adulteress.' 'Sinner.' 'Kill her!'

Jesus, who had seated himself in a circle of his followers, turned to look at the new-comers. Ezra spoke to him with assumed respect. 'Master,' he said, 'what should we do? This woman has been caught in the act of adultery. She should be punished according to the Law. What do you say?'

Legally, Ezra was right. According to the Law (Deuteronomy 22: 13–24), the penalty for adultery in the case of a betrothed girl was death. She and the guilty partner must be taken outside the city gates and stoned. So, legally speaking, there was only one answer to Ezra's question. 'Answer, Master,' said Eliphaz eagerly, 'we want to know your opinion.' Other voices joined in.

Jesus took his time. He bent down and seemed to be writing with his finger in the dust on the earth. At length he looked up and spoke. 'If anyone among you is without sin, let him throw the first stone.' There was silence. The woman looked at Jesus with hope. Slowly, the people dropped the stones that they had taken up. Jesus resumed his writing in the dust. The adulteress, freed from the grip of her tormentors, remained motionless, her head bowed down. Jesus looked at her. 'Where are your accusers?' he said. 'Is there anyone who had condemned you?' 'No, Lord,' she answered, 'no one.' Jesus spoke gravely but gently. 'Then neither do I condemn you. Go and sin no more.'

Outside the city gates the Nazareth caravan had just arrived. Among its members were Rabbi Yehuda now a very old man, and Mary, the mother of Jesus. 'Our feet shall stand within thy gates, O Jerusalem', Yehuda said. Then to Mary, in a low voice, 'Your son will be teaching in the Temple. Shall I take you to him?' But Mary said, 'No, I will wait. I will see him when it is time.'

The next day a crowd again gathered in the Temple colonnade around Jesus. They were watching him as he anointed the eyes of a blind man with a paste made of dust mixed with spittle.

Unable to see Jesus the blind man called out again. 'Leave my eyes alone! I don't want them touched I tell you.'

Some of the crowd joined in his protest.

'Yes, leave him alone.'

'Why are they smearing that stuff on his eyes? He doesn't want them touched.'

Jesus refrained from answering. He finished anointing the man's eyes and then, speaking as one with authority, instructed him, 'Go and wash your eyes'.

Surrounded by a number of curious onlookers, the blind man was led off, although most of the people remained behind with Jesus.

Peter asked him, 'Master, the man was born blind, and what I should like to know is this. Who sinned? Did he sin, or was it his father, or his mother?' For it was the Jewish belief that there could be no suffering without sin.

'No one sinned', said Jesus. 'He was born blind so that the will of God might be made manifest in him. I must perform the work of him who sent me, so long as daylight lasts. Then the night will fall, in which no man may work. But as long as I am in the world, I am the light of the world.'

The blind man went to the pool and washed, and his sight returned. He looked round at the visible world with fear, but with a kind of timid joy also. The crowd began shouting, 'He sees – he's been given his sight! Blind from birth, and now he can see!'

A group of Pharisees tried to check this new wave of popularity for Jesus. When a man shouted, 'How did this happen? How was it done?', a Pharisee turned to the blind man himself and asked, "And what do *you* say? What do you have to say about the man who healed you?'

'He is a prophet', said the blind man. 'There is no doubt.'

'What are you saying?' said the Pharisee. 'You got your sight back from God, not from that man. He is a sinner.'

The blind man was frightened by the outstretched fists of the Pharisees and shrank back, thus coming close to Jesus, who stood in the midst of his followers. 'Do you believe in the Son of Man?', Jesus asked him quietly.

'Who is he, Master,' said the blind man, 'that I may believe in him?'

'You are seeing him', said Jesus. 'It is he who is speaking to you.'

'I believe, Lord', said the blind man.

Whereupon a Pharisee said to Jesus, 'And what is your story – that you can give sight to blind people?'

Jesus addressed the crowd. 'I came into this world to give sight to those who cannot see, and to take away sight from those who can.'

'What do you mean by this?' demanded another Pharisee. 'Do you mean that we who are righteous are blind?'

'If you were blind,' said Jesus, 'you would be without sin, but since you claim to see, your sin remains.' 'This man works through the devil!' a Pharisee shouted. 'Why do you listen to him?'

The crowd rapidly increased at the prospect of a row, and began to take sides in the controversy.

'What do you mean – mad?'

'Can the mad restore sight?'

'Can devils make men who are blind see God's daylight?'

'No, it's true – if his power is not from God, it must be from the other one.'

'Shut your ears, don't listen to him!' The Pharisees were succeeding in rousing the crowd against Jesus. The tumult was growing worse. Jesus therefore climbed on to a rock and attacked the group of Pharisees. 'Alas for you, scribes and Pharisees', said Jesus. 'You hypocrites! You who shut up the Kingdom of Heaven in men's faces, neither going in yourselves nor allowing others to go in. Alas for you, blind guides who strain out gnats and swallow camels. You who bow before the letter of the Law and violate the heart of the Law – justice, mercy, good faith! Alas for you, scribes and Pharisees, you who are like whited sepulchres, fair without, but inside full of dead men's bones and every kind of corruption. Serpents, brood of vipers, how can you escape damnation?'

For some moments Zerah had been an unobtrusive observer of the scene, and at that moment he decided in his heart that Jesus must die. But Jesus had not yet finished. 'Yours is a house of desolation,' he said, 'the home of the lizard and the spider. And this I say to you – you will not see me here again until you have learned to cry with a loud voice "Blessed is he who comes in the name of the Lord!" Because I and my Father are one and the same.' Zerah was furious.

At these words, there were angry cries.

'Blasphemer!'

'He blasphemed!'

'Stone him!'

'He is a false prophet!'

194

Other voices were shouting, 'No, he speaks truly!' 'Leave him!' 'Let him go!'

The disciples surrounded Jesus, offering him protection, while the Pharisees incited the crowd against him. 'Seize him!' they shouted. 'Why hesitate? He blasphemes against law and religion. He is a friend of sinners and thieves and whores! From his own mouth he condemns himself. Stone him! Throw him out of the holy city!'

A man in the crowd shouted, 'Throw yourselves out! You whited sepulchres!'

Barabbas emerged from the excited crowd. He shouted, 'Yes, yes, stone the traitor, Caesar's friend, licker of Caesar's feet!' He and his Zealots started throwing stones, and a scrimmage began. A party of Roman guards arrived to restore order, and in the struggle Barabbas seized one of the guards. Some of the Zealots, including Barabbas, were roughly arrested. The Temple party, who had been looking on, hurried away.

Barabbas was marched into the Antonia Fortress and thrown into a cell already occupied by two other Jewish criminals, Joah and Aram. Beyond the fortress Zealots were shouting for his release. Their cries could be faintly heard in the cell and Barabbas, knowing such demonstrations to be useless, listened in stony silence. After a short interval the warden admitted an attendant named Quintus, who was bringing a dish of food and was accompanied by a guard named Quartus.

'Your friends outside want you freed. So that you can carry on with your murdering, I suppose', Quintus said banteringly.

'I'm not a murderer', Barabbas protested. 'I'm a patriot, and shouldn't be in the same cell as that lot', and he gestured scornfully toward Joah and Aram.

'You're all criminals,' Quintus observed cheerfully,' and are likely to share the same fate. So don't think you're any different, my fine patriot.'

Towards sunset that evening Jesus and his disciples were in the Garden of Gethsemane on the Mount of Olives. They had withdrawn there because after the riot in which the Zealots had been arrested the city had become dangerous. They were grouped round Jesus, talking quietly, when an elderly Pharisee came up the hill into the garden, plainly looking for someone. He paused for a moment to regain his breath after the long hill climb. Then he recognized Peter and came over to him.

'You will remember me, Nicodemus. And you know you can trust me. I've come to warn you, and to offer my help. You're in danger, very real danger. Tell your Master to keep out of public places – to keep right out of sight.' Then he picked out Jesus and turned to him.

'Rabbi,' he said, 'there is to be a meeting of the Sanhedrin. You have many enemies there, but friends also who know that you are a teacher come from God, for no man can work your miracles unless God is with him. Yet, my heart is still troubled and my mind confused. You must help me to see the truth.'

'Except a man be born again from above,' Jesus said to Nicodemus, 'he cannot see the Kingdom of God.' 'How can a man be born again?' said Nicodemus, puzzled. 'Can he enter his mother's womb a second time?' Jesus answered, 'I tell you, and it is true, unless a man is born of water and the Spirit, he cannot become a member of the Kingdom of God. Physical birth can only beget a physical creature; but spiritual birth begets a spiritual creature. You must not be surprised that I said to you that you must all be born again from above. The wind blows where it wills, and you hear the sound of it but do not know where it comes from nor where it is going. And there is the same invisible and unpredictable power in everyone who undergoes this spiritual rebirth. The light came into the world but men prefer darkness.'

'How can this be?', asked Nicodemus.

'God so loved the world,' said Jesus, 'that he sent his own son, that whosoever believed in him should not perish but have eternal life. God sent his son into the world not to condemn the world but that it might be saved through him.'

Nicodemus was moved and troubled. 'Master,' he said, 'I beg you, take care. Too many hate you.' In a low voice Jesus quoted, 'He was despised and rejected of men. A man of sorrows and acquainted with grief . . . And we hid as it were our faces from him . . .'

'That's Isaiah, Master', Nicodemus said.

'Old words,' Jesus said to Nicodemus, 'but not much time will pass before they become new again, and then perhaps you will be reborn.'

The same evening, selected members of the Sanhedrin assembled in a council chamber of the Temple, having been hastily summoned to a very secret meeting, Zerah the Sadducee was present, as were Pharisees Nicodemus and Joseph of Arimathea. The attitude of the members was secretive, almost furtive.

The meeting was presided over by the High Priest, Caiaphas, and he sat leaning forward, his eyes half closed. Although members of the Sanhedrin specifically addressed him, he neither answered nor raised his gaze to attend. He seemed either bored with the business or too absorbed in his own thoughts to take notice. As a consequence everyone redoubled their efforts to attract his attention.

'The city is in uproar', said Haggai. 'One group of rebels has been arrested already, and more Roman troops are arriving from Caesarea.'

'Our information', said Samuel, 'is that this Jesus of Nazareth will use the Passover festival to declare himself the Son of David. The mob already calls him a prophet. I appeal to our High Priest Lord Caiaphas . . .'

Joseph of Arimathea broke in, 'I don't believe it. I have seen Jesus. I have heard him preach. He talks of goodness and the virtues of poverty . . .'

'And hence of the vices of the rich and the hypocrisy of the respectable', Haggai broke in. 'We all know about the virtues of the respectable', said Joseph of Arimathea. 'We can imagine what a sincere teacher like Jesus must think of them . . .'

'A sincere teacher!' exclaimed Habbakuk, appalled. 'He is a false teacher and is not even original. He says nothing new. We've heard it all before, from John the Baptist, from hundreds of others.'

'Jesus of Nazareth', said Samuel, 'inflames the mob and the Zealots, who regard him as the new King of Israel who can sweep out the Romans.'

'But again and again he says that his kingdom is not of this world', objected Joseph of Arimathea.

'Indeed he does', sneered Ezra. 'He merely says *he* is the fulfilment of God's promise. The completion of our entire history. I tell you,' he cried angrily, 'he outrages the law of our Fathers. His guilt is blasphemy.'

The atmosphere was becoming more and more heated, and Nicodemus now spoke. 'I submit with all respect that we must also consider the possibility that Jesus of Nazareth *is* the Messiah awaited by our people.'

The interjection led to a moment of appalled silence.

'A carpenter from Galilee?', shrilled Habbakuk. 'Riding into Jerusalem on a donkey! Just to fulfil the prophecy?'

'Like our brother Joseph,' said Nicodemus, 'I have heard him preach. I was moved and I saw wonders . . . signs that God may be with him.'

'Have a care, Master Nicodemus', said Habbakuk. 'You have heard only oratory. You have only seen magic that comes from the devil.' 'The coming of the Messiah', said Nicodemus, 'is the core of our faith. Why should he not come now? Why do we dream that our liberator will be a new Solomon or a new David? Is God not allowed to choose the son of a carpenter from Nazareth? David was a shepherd. Who are we to decide the way in which God should choose to help his people? We are grains of sand. We are chaff blown in the wind. May the Lord God open our eyes to his wisdom.'

Predictably his words produced an angry outcry. 'Who says that Jesus is not dangerous, when people in our very midst defend him?' cried Samuel, and many speakers started shouting in chorus, until they suddenly realized that the High Priest was holding up his hand for silence.

The authority of Caiaphas, like his sincerity, was beyond question. 'Brethren,' he said, 'I am an old man and, like Master Nicodemus, I am deeply troubled. My heart is sore wounded. How can we have reached such divisions and bitterness? This rabbi from Nazareth must be an exceptional man . . .' Habbakuk was about to interrupt but Caiaphas checked him with a gesture. 'Please listen, brethren', he went on. 'Never before has the Sanhedrin been so divided. Why? How has Jesus of Nazareth managed to do this to us? In what does he differ from other prophets and rabbis of our two thousand years of history? I will tell you, brethren. He differs in that he says that he has the power to forgive sins. We have always believed that only God has the power to do that. What does it then mean if this man Jesus takes to himself the power to forgive sins? I hardly dare utter the thought. It means that a carpenter from Nazareth identifies himself with God. This desperate sin happened only once before. Only one creature dared that, and his name was Lucifer. Brethren! Master Joseph! Master Nicodemus! Can we accept his claim? Can a man be equal to God?' Nicodemus was about to speak, but checked himself and remained silent. 'Our scriptures tell us', continued Caiaphas, 'that the Messiah will come as a king. Is this man a king? If he is not, is he a blasphemer? What is the truth in him for which we are to reject two thousand years of teaching and endanger the lives of our people? This is the question that devastates my heart. The Romans will not wait long for us to answer. At the first whisper of revolt they will begin slaughtering the people. We cannot allow our people to die for a false Messiah. We must decide, we must act, in haste. If Jesus is a false prophet, should one man die for the good of the people? Should the nation perish for one man?'

'Lord Caiaphas,' Zerah broke in, 'may I remind you with respect that the people of Israel may put a goat to death but not a man.' As an occupied country Israel was not allowed to carry out the death penalty. The Sanhedrin could pronounce a man guilty and condemn him to death but the sentence could be carried out only by the Romans at their own discretion.

'Thank you, Zerah', said Caiaphas. 'I wondered when I should hear from you. You remind us of the limits to our justice. We may formulate a charge. The Romans must execute it.'

'For us,' said Zerah, 'this Jesus is guilty of blasphemy: for the Romans it would have to be treason.'

'Guilty?' Joseph of Arimathea broke in. 'Do you have proof that he is guilty?'

'Yes', said Zerah. 'I heard him in the Temple. He claimed to be the Son of God. That merits death.'

'Surely, my Lord,' said Nicodemus, 'the Sanhedrin has always been reluctant to pass death sentences. And does our law condemn a man without first giving him a hearing before the elders of Israel?'

'No, Master Nicodemus,' answered Caiaphas, 'it does not. We must question the man and give him every opportunity to explain himself.'

The formal part of the meeting was now over, and most of the members left. But at the request of Caiaphas a small group remained to consider how best Jesus could be brought before the Sanhedrin for questioning.

'We must arrest him', said Zerah.

'No', said Joseph of Arimathea.

'Let me persuade him', said Nicodemus.

'We must take him in darkness,' said Zerah, 'to avoid a riot. There are always too many people around him.'

'My Lord?' Nicodemus broke in, but Caiaphas said, 'I would like to follow your advice, Nicodemus, but I believe that Zerah is right.' Zerah was about to leave, but Caiaphas checked him. 'Zerah', said Caiaphas.

'My Lord?', said Zerah.

'Do not forget that he is one of our brothers.'

It was late when Zerah met Judas, who was standing waiting for him in the Court of Israel. He looked downcast and tired.

'Ah, Judas', said Zerah. 'I'm glad you came, I've been trying to get in touch with you. You haven't been with the Master for the last day or two. Where have you been?'

'I have been trying to think, Zerah,' said Judas, 'trying to decide what to do.'

'You seemed to me to be a man who was very sure of himself and of what to do', said Zerah.

'I'm not now', said Judas. 'I'm confused. I always thought that a sanction from the Sanhedrin could solve everything. I thought that I should think clearly and then act clearly.'

'That's right,' said Zerah, 'a cool head and a strong will.'

'The Master told me', said Judas, 'that the heart is more important. He doesn't need my ideas. I'm tormented by the fear that he's right. *Have* I hardened my heart? Am I fit to be one of his disciples?' There was a long pause.

'Judas,' said Zerah, 'don't lie to yourself. The truth is that in your heart you no longer

198

believe that Jesus of Nazareth *is* the Messiah. You no longer believe his claim to fulfil the scriptures. You are torn by doubts.' Zerah looked hard at Judas, and Judas's eyes fell before him. 'Judas,' he said, 'there is only one way to know the truth. Hand Jesus over to the Sanhedrin.' Judas looked up. Zerah smiled reassuringly. 'Think, Judas', he said. 'Many influential members of the Council admire Jesus. He will be fairly judged. If he is the Messiah God will not abandon him. If he is not . . . if he is only another false prophet . . . you and I will have saved Israel.' There was a silence while the two men looked at each other. Then Zerah said as he turned away, 'The Sanhedrin will be very grateful to you'.

The Passover was the greatest of the annual festivals which every adult male who lived within 15 miles of Jerusalem had to attend. Its origin went back to the supreme moment in the national history, when a reluctant Pharaoh was compelled by a succession of disastrous plagues to allow the enslaved Israelites to go free. Time and again Pharaoh 'hardened his heart', until a last and most terrible plague broke his resistance. The angel of death passed through the land and slew the firstborn of every Egyptian household.

Warned by God of the visitation in advance, the Israelites were ordered to dip a branch of hyssop into the blood of a newly slain lamb, and smear the doorposts and lintels of their houses. When the angel of death saw the blood he would 'pass over' the house, leaving its inmates unscathed; hence the name of the feast, which is still celebrated by the Jews on the 14th day of Nisan (approximately 14th April).

Many symbolic ingredients made up the feast, and were consumed in the course of an impressive ritual which included prayer, the singing of psalms, and the recital of the history of Israel up to the great deliverance.

Wine was taken at four stages in the meal, as a reminder of the four promises of God concerning delivery from bondage, and the unique status of the Israelites as the chosen people.

Bread was broken as a reminder that slaves had only broken crusts to eat, never a whole loaf.

Bitter herbs placed between two pieces of unleavened bread recalled the bitterness of slavery and the bread their fathers had eaten when escaping from Egypt. These were dipped into the *charosheth*, a paste made of dates, apples, nuts and pomegranates to symbolize the clay of which their enslaved fathers had been compelled to make bricks. The dipped bread was called the sop.

The chief ingredient of the feast was of course the whole lamb, a reminder of the slain lamb whose sprinkled blood preserved Jewish households when the angel of death passed through Egypt. A minimum of ten celebrants was required at the festival in any one house, and whatever remained of the lamb had to be destroyed. It must not be kept over and used at an ordinary meal.

This was the Passover feast which Jesus took and made his own. The two parts which he must have made specially his own were the breaking of bread and the cup of wine. To this part of the ceremony Jesus added his own explanation. He must have said something like this, 'Blessed art thou, O Lord our God, who has blessed us with thy laws and made bread issue from the earth.' Then he must have gone on, 'From this moment this bread will no longer be the bread of the passage of our fathers from bondage to freedom. For this is my body, which enters into death for you. From this moment on, do this in remembrance of me. This Passover, memorial of the bondage in Egypt, is for you today the passage from the bondage of death to the freedom of life. This is the bread of life. Whoever eats of this bread shall have eternal life.'

Clearly, a new revelation was given to the apostles in these words.

Then Peter said, 'Lord, we are happy to eat this Passover with you'.

And Jesus answered gravely, 'Truly, I tell you, one of you is about to betray me'. The disciples were torn between consternation and disbelief. Peter expressed their dismay.

'I speak for us all, Master, when I say that none here could as much as dream of betraying you. Do you mean that evil will take possession of one of us?'

'I know those whom I have chosen,' said Jesus, 'but the scripture must be fulfilled.'

John, who was sitting next to Jesus, whispered to him, 'Lord, tell me who will betray you'. And Jesus whispered back, 'He who dips his bread in the plate when I dip mine'.

Just then, Judas dipped his bread in the *charosheth*. John looked in horror, but he kept silent. And Jesus said quietly, 'Judas, what you are going to do, do it quickly'. Thereupon Judas got up and went out.

An apostle asked his neighbour, 'Where is he going?' And his companion answered, 'The Master told him to do something'.

Then came the last cup of the feast. As Jesus raised it he said, 'Now the son of man is risen and enters into glory. All will be gathered unto him. I shall not be with you much longer. You will look for me . . . but where I am going, you cannot come.'

At this Peter was unable to restrain himself. 'Master,' he said, 'I will follow you wherever you go.'

'No, Peter,' said Jesus, 'now you cannot follow me. You will follow me later. Truly, I tell you, all of you will abandon me.'

'Never, never, I swear, never', said Peter. 'Why do you say such things? I will never deny you.'

'Peter,' Jesus said, 'before the cock crows tomorrow you will have denied me three times. Remember my words.'

'Never,' Peter cried again, 'never!'

Jesus looked round his disciples. 'If I do not leave,' he said, 'the Holy Spirit cannot descend upon you. Greater love hath no man than this, that a man lay down his life for a friend. By this shall all men know that you are my disciples, if you love one another. I am the way, the truth and the life. From now on the cup will not only be a memorial and sacrament of the covenant that God made with our fathers on Mount Sinai. This cup which is poured out for you is the new covenant in my blood. Do this in memory of me. You will thus share my death and my resurrection. As the branch cannot bear fruit by itself, but only as it abides in the vine, so neither can you unless you abide in me. I am the vine. You are the branches. He who abides in me, and I in him, he it is who bears much fruit, for apart from me you can do nothing.' The emotional atmosphere became more intense as Jesus, looking upward, said, 'Father, the hour has come. Glorify thy son, that the son may glorify thee. Thou hast given him power to give eternal life, which is to know thee, the only true God, and Jesus Christ whom thou hast sent. Father, keep in thy name those whom thou hast given me. Sanctify them in the truth. Thy word is truth. As thou didst send me into the world, so I have sent them into the world that hates them. For their sake, I consecrate myself, that they also may be consecrated in truth. I do not pray for these only, but also for all who believe in me through their word, that they may all be one, even as thou, Father, art in me and I in thee, so also may they be in us, that the world may believe that thou hast sent me.'

The meal was drawn to its close with the quiet singing of the 136th Psalm, and anxiety and sadness were for the moment forgotten in the fervency of prayer.

After the meal Jesus led his disciples to the Garden of Gethsemane. The garden was an orchard enclosed on two sides by a high wall, with the other two sides bounded by a deep ravine. There was almost a full moon, and its brilliancy lit up the scene as though it were daylight. Jesus and the apostles approached the orchard, and a boy named Mark opened a little gate in the wall to admit them and remained on watch by the gate after they had entered.

Jesus spoke to the disciples. 'The hour is near when you shall all be scattered, each on his own, and you will leave me.'

'Lord,' Peter said, 'I am ready to follow you to the death.'

'Three times, Peter,' said Jesus, 'before the first cock crows. Remember. My soul is heavy with sorrow, even unto death. Keep watch while I pray.'

He went forward a little way and dropped on his knees. The apostles were uncertain whether to go with him, but Peter, with a gesture, bade them stop.

Then Jesus prayed, 'My God, my God, why hast thou forsaken me? I call thee by day and thou dost not answer, by night and I have no peace. Do not stay far from me, as my anguish is near and none can help me.' He fell on his face. Andrew, John and Peter were watching. Andrew exclaimed, 'Look at the – sweat.' John said, 'It's not sweat. It's . . .' Peter exclaimed, 'Oh, my dear Lord!'

Jesus continued in anguished prayer, and the disciples, their eyes heavy with watching, fell asleep. At length Jesus stood up. The bright moonlight showed the boy Mark by the gate, also asleep, and a shadow passed over him. Then Jesus went up to Peter and laid his hand on his shoulder to waken him. 'So,' he said, 'you had not the strength to keep awake with me for one hour. The spirit is willing, but the flesh is weak.' Peter, startled, shook the others awake. 'Behold,' said Jesus, 'the hour has come when the Son of Man is to be betrayed into the hands of sinners.'

The wind was rising and clouds appeared in the sky. From beyond the wall there was a sound of voices. 'Wake up, boy', a guard called roughly. 'Let us through.'

'There's no one here', said Mark terrified.

'So much the better,' said the guard's voice, 'but we shall see.'

'Let go! Let me go! Help!', the boy shouted.

The disciples were thrown into disorder. 'What's happening?' they called to one another. 'We've been betrayed.'

'These men are not Romans.'

'Quick, there may be a gate on the other side.'

Some of the apostles ran across the clearing, then they stopped and returned, realizing that Jesus had not moved and that Peter, John and Matthew were retracing their steps and going back to him. A group of men guided by Judas appeared in the garden. Judas went straight up to Jesus and kissed him on the cheek. 'Master', said Judas.

Jesus stared at him. 'This is your hour, Judas,' he said, 'the hour of shadows. You betray your Master with a kiss.' Judas looked at him, confused and troubled.

Zerah pointed out Jesus to the guards. 'That's the man', he said. 'Arrest him.'

The guards moved forward to seize Jesus. Andrew and Peter threw themselves on Judas. 'You planned this. You dog. You traitor. You planned it from the start!' Andrew struck Judas on the face.

Judas, with the strength of despair, held Andrew by the wrists. 'You ignorant fisherman! Why can't you use your brains.' He pushed Andrew away and grabbed Peter. 'Peter,' he pleaded, 'listen. Surely you can understand that if he is the Messiah he will triumph. The only way to help him is to force him to speak to the Sanhedrin. He has friends there. Let them escort him to Caiaphas.'

'Never!' cried Peter. 'If they take him, he won't come back.'

'Peter', said Judas. 'Do you really believe in him?' But Peter had turned to attack the guards, who had already bound Jesus's wrists. He gave one guard's ear a glancing wound with his knife. Jesus in a commanding voice stopped him. 'No, Peter,' he ordered, 'put your dagger down.'

Peter was perplexed by the calmness of Jesus. He began to think that just possibly what Judas had said was true. There was a moment of great confusion. Zerah called for the other guards who had remained outside the wall. 'Arrest them all!'

Jesus checked him. 'It was me you sought', he said. 'Now you have found me, let them go!' In a moment the garden, the scene of so much commotion, was almost deserted. The disciples ran away. Jesus was marched out by the guards, Zerah leading.

Once they had gone, the disciples, slowly and furtively, began to emerge from their hiding places. They drew together, confused and frightened,

'They were Temple guards', Philip whispered.

'They'll have taken him to the High Priest', Matthew added.

'Judas', muttered Andrew, 'said it was to save him.'

'*He said*!' John interjected. 'He was the betrayer. The Master knew he was betraying him.'

'Nicodemus warned us', Peter said bitterly. 'He warned us.'

'We had better separate', Philip said, 'Some of us should go and find out where he is.'

'We must remember to keep well out of sight', said Matthew. 'We are all in danger now.'

'No, I am going after the Master', said Peter. 'What Judas said might be true.'

Very early the next morning, Judas, desperately agitated, entered the courtyard of Caiaphas's house. A guard opened a door and looked out through the crack. Judas shouted to the guard, 'Where have they taken him? Where's Zerah? I must speak with Zerah the priest'. He saw the door closing and rushed over to it. He beat on it with his fists. The guard opened the door slightly and looked out again. 'Is he here?' demanded

Judas. 'Did they bring him here? Call the priest for me, Zerah.'

The first man called to a second guard who was in the courtyard, 'Here, throw him out!' He closed the door and the guard in the courtyard approached Judas. 'You hear', he said. 'Get out.' He tried to get hold of Judas to throw him out and Judas cried out again. 'I must speak to Zerah. Don't you understand? Make him come out to me.'

The main door of the house opened and Zerah stepped out followed by a group of priests and a guard. He walked through the door at which Judas had been knocking minutes before. Judas ran up to him. 'Zerah,' he said, 'at last. Where is the meeting with the Lord Caiaphas? I must be there with Jesus.'

'Meeting?' said Zerah. 'There is no meeting.'

'What?' cried Judas.

'There's an investigation', said Zerah. 'Your Jesus had to answer many questions.'

Judas stared at him in horror. 'I did wrong', he said, 'to deliver him to you. His blood is innocent.'

Zerah answered, 'You helped Israel, Judas. You deserve our gratitude.' He started to leave but stopped, and turning with an apologetic smile put a bag of money into Judas's hands. 'I hope', he said, 'you won't be offended by this. This is for your services.' And he walked away quickly, followed by his men.

Judas remained standing motionless, the bag in his hand.

'That's enough now', said the guard. 'You've got what you wanted, haven't you? So now get out of here', and he seized Judas by the arm.

There was a frenzied knocking at the door of Joseph of Arimathea's house. The door opened and Joseph looked out anxiously. It was Rabbi Yehuda, the Nazareth rabbi, who was knocking, while Mary stood a little way off. The two men spoke rapidly in great agitation.

'I am sorry', said Rabbi Yehuda, 'to waken you at this hour.'

'I was up', answered Joseph.

'Jesus of Nazareth has been arrested', Rabbi Yehuda said. 'His mother and I . . .'

Joseph of Arimathea broke in, 'I know! I have been summoned to a meeting. I will do everything I can.'

Men by this time were running through the streets of Jerusalem. Judas ran along frantically. Joseph of Arimathea was also hurrying to the High Priest's house. Peter was slinking furtively along by a wall inside the city.

In the country outside Jerusalem the pale light of the early sun threw long shadows. It cast one shadow which moved rhythmically, forwards then backwards. Some coins glinted on the ground and seemed in their brightness to be greeting the morning light. The returning shadow dimmed their brightness for a moment then let them shine again as the body of Judas, suspended from the tree, swung lazily to and fro.

4

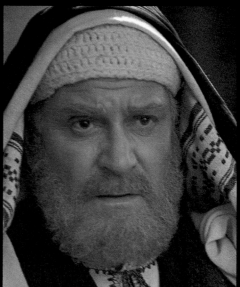

19

PART 6

THE PROPHECY
FULFILLED

PHOTOGRAPHS

1 Caiaphas rose and solemnly rent his priestly robe

2 'No,' declared Peter, in a sudden fright, 'I have no idea what you're talking about'

3 'Is this your dangerous aspirant to kingship?' Pilate asked. 'Tattered, barefoot, emaciated'

4 'What is truth?', said Pilate, and looked at Jesus in some perplexity. 'Who are you?' he asked

5 The flogging was carried out with a long leathern whip, studded at intervals with pellets of lead

6 'But he said he was the King of the Jews,' a centurion protested. 'Surely we ought to attire him as befits his rank'

7 'Behold the man!'

8 Pilate looked at Jesus. He stood quietly watching the crowd, giving no outward sign of anxiety or despair

9 'Very well', said Pilate. 'They want Barabbas. They shall have Barabbas'

10 'I'm sick of the whole business,' said Pilate, 'and wish I'd never seen this Jesus'

11 In intense pain and weakness Jesus began the walk to Calvary

12 A woman emerged from the crowd and mercifully wiped the sweat and blood from his face

13 Jesus lay on the ground as his hands were nailed to the cross-piece, to which he was also bound

14 Then he was hoisted up

15 Pilate's sign had gone up over the cross, 'Jesus of Nazareth, King of the Jews'

16 Mary, the mother of Jesus, and Martha made their way to the foot of the cross

17 His mother looking at his lifeless, rainwashed body gave vent to a terrible flood of grief

18 Mary Magdalene and the sisters Martha and Mary were walking timidly toward the tomb when a sentry ordered them to halt

19 Zerah arranged to have the tomb guarded

20 Zerah stood inside the empty tomb. 'Now it begins', he muttered. 'Now it all begins. . .'

21 'Peter, Matthew, all of you,' cried Mary Magdalene, 'I've seen him. I've seen the Master!'

22 The disciples turned to look and Jesus stood there silhouetted in the doorway

Daylight would not be long in coming now.

The servants and Temple guards standing round the fire in the courtyard to Caiaphas's house, watched with idle interest as members of the Sanhedrin hurried up to the great portico, some importantly, others with tense anxious faces.

In the house, in the servants' hall, a detachment of soldiers with time on their hands and Jesus at their mercy had invented a mocking game. Having blindfolded the prisoner they one by one crept up and punched him, now here, now there, then to roars of appreciative laughter they called out, 'Prophesy now, who hit you?'

The rough sport was interrupted by the entrance of Zerah. He looked on coldly for a few minutes, then, without a word being spoken, a soldier stepped forward and removed the blindfold. 'You can untie his hands too', Zerah snapped. When the order had been carried out he indicated with a curt jerk of his head that Jesus was to follow him. With similar terse signalling he told off four of the Temple guards to accompany them, and led the way out through the servants' entrance across the courtyard to the great portico.

Peter had made his way into the courtyard, and was feeling isolated, lonely, chilly, and decidedly out of his depth in the precincts of the great house and in the company of its knowing retainers. With a clutch of fear he saw Jesus emerge with the soldiers and pass silently across the courtyard, to disappear again into the great house. He started to shiver and began to edge his way toward the fire.

Zerah led his small party until they reached an imposing assembly room. Here Caiaphas was seated flanked on one side by Sadducees and on the other by Pharisees, among whom were Nicodemus and Joseph of Arimathea. Zerah placed Jesus, standing, before the High Priest, with a Temple guard on either side. These arrangements completed, he took his place at the table, next to the High Priest.

It was an investigation they were conducting, not a formal trial, and the approach of Caiaphas was at the beginning quite disarming. 'Rabbi,' he said to Jesus, 'we have brought you here so that you can answer for yourself. There have been charges of blasphemy. Remembering that, we want you to think very carefully before answering our questions. And the first question, indeed the key question, is simply this: What is the nature of the doctrine that you and your disciples have been spreading here in Judea?'

'My lord Caiaphas,' Jesus answered, 'I have spoken openly for all the world to hear. I have taught daily in the Temple where Jews from the whole country meet together. I have said nothing in secret. Those who have heard me are my witnesses.'

At this display of firmness one of the guards, hoping to ingratiate himself with his superiors by a show of righteous indignation, aimed a blow at Jesus. 'Is that the way to answer the High Priest?', he demanded.

Nicodemus at once protested. 'My Lord,' he cried, 'the man exceeds his duty. His conduct is most unseemly. Most unseemly.'

'I agree', said Caiaphas. 'His action was quite unwarranted', and turning to the guard he said, 'You are dismissed. Leave the council chamber'. Surlily crestfallen the man went out. Another guard stepped into his place and Caiaphas turned again to Jesus. 'Please continue, Rabbi', he said courteously.

'If I have done anything wrong,' said Jesus, 'make a charge against me. If I have not, then why am I being held?'

His defiant attitude disturbed his friends, and seeing their anxiety his opponents became more assured. They began to press charges.

'My Lord Caiaphas', Haggai the Sadducee called out in a loud assertive voice. 'There are witnesses who will testify that he said he would destroy the Temple and build it again in three days.'

'I heard him myself', confirmed Zerah speaking in low confidential tones to the High Priest.

'But no man could say such a thing and mean it literally', Nicodemus objected. 'Whatever was said about rebuilding the Temple must have had a symbolic meaning.'

'No, no, and again no!' another Pharisee cried excitedly. 'He said he would destroy the Temple, and those who heard him knew that he meant exactly what he said. He would destroy the Temple. Then after four days he would rebuild it.'

'Three days? Four days?' said Joseph of Arimathea. 'The witnesses disagree.'

'How can we remember every last detail!', said Haggai. 'There was a riot which Jesus himself provoked, but for which the Romans will hold us responsible.'

'The riot', Nicodemus reminded him, 'was caused by Barabbas.'

'But Barabbas was provoked to violence by the shocking blasphemy of the accused', said Zerah. 'Who can say how many more devout Jews he will provoke by his preaching? And every disturbance provides the Romans with another excuse to attack our people.'

'Yes, we all know what the Romans have done to our people', said Joseph of Arimathea. 'Our people have been nailed to the very walls of Jerusalem because there were not scaffolds enough to satisfy the Roman lust for blood. We cannot enter our holy city without the stench of Jewish victims assaulting our nostrils. Let us indeed think carefully about the way the Romans treat our people. Do any of us here wish to give Pontius Pilate another victim if we can prevent it?'

'I must revert to my former question', said the High Priest. 'What exactly is the nature of our brother's teaching?' They all looked at Jesus. The crucial moment had come. With great solemnity Caiaphas addressed him. 'In the name of the living God, I adjure you to tell us if you are indeed the Christ, the Son of God.'

Jesus answered, 'I am'.

The reply was so sensational that it stunned the whole assembly into momentary silence. His friends were utterly dismayed. He had himself deliberately closed the door of hope. His enemies, though appalled by his blasphemy, were secretly delighted by his folly. The claim, so openly made, was so unequivocal that there could now be no escape. They could proceed against him with a good conscience and with every prospect of attaining their end.

From every side cries of 'Blasphemy' and 'Away with him' went up. 'We need hear

236

no more', said Caiaphas, but Jesus had not finished.

'And you shall see the Son of God sitting at the right hand of the Power of God and coming in the clouds of heaven', he said.

Caiaphas rose and solemnly rent his priestly robe, whether ceremonially at the blasphemy, or in despair at Jesus's obstinacy, those who witnessed the act could not decide. Zerah, anxious to take immediate advantage of the situation, gave them no time to reflect. 'We have all heard him', he said in rapid, decisive tones. 'He has condemned himself. For such blasphemy there can be but one penalty. Death. We must take him to Pilate to have the death penalty confirmed. But first we must formulate suitable charges against him. Take him away,' he said, turning to the guards, 'and hold him in safe custody.'

Jesus was accordingly taken out and led back, through the courtyard to the soldiers' quarters. Peter, who had edged his way cautiously right up to the fire, and was warming himself with the servants, once more saw Jesus silently pass. Something in his look as his eyes followed Jesus arrested the attention of one of the maidservants. 'You were with him, weren't you?' she asked.

'No,' declared Peter, in a sudden fright, 'I have no idea what you're talking about.' And he heard a cock crow.

'You speak like someone from Galilee,' said another maid, her curiosity aroused. 'Surely you must be one of his disciples.'

Peter's voice grew strident. 'I've already told you I know nothing whatever about the man', and he began calling down curses on himself if he was not telling the truth. And again the cock crew.

The maid stared at him. Tears forced themselves into his eyes. He rushed from the courtyard and his weeping became uncontrollable.

And for the third time the cock crew.

It was always a matter of keen regret for Pilate to have to leave the civilized comforts and amusements of Caesarea, his Roman capital for the administration of Palestine, to take up residence in the dreary Jewish capital. At Passover time especially, Jerusalem was at its fanatical worst, and as he reached the outskirts of the city his gloom and irritability increased.

Once inside the fortress Pilate lost no time in reaching the comfort of his private apartments. He was welcomed by Quintilius, the Deputy Procurator and fortress commander responsible for order in Jerusalem.

'Who is this Barabbas?' Pilate asked, 'the mob yelled his name at me on my way here.'

'He was arrested for public disaffection', Quintilius answered. 'His death warrant awaits your signature.'

'What was his crime?'

'He is a Zealot. He smashed a Roman standard and killed one of our auxiliaries.'

'Is he popular?', Pilate asked.

'Very, with the Jewish rabble.'

'A friend of the Sanhedrin?', Pilate asked.

'Far from it', said Quintilius.

'Can we use the incident to our advantage?'

'It is customary to release a prisoner in celebration of the Passover.'

'Should Barabbas be the man?', asked Pilate.

'Are you tired of the stench of executions?', asked Quintilius.

'Should Barabbas be the man?', Pilate repeated irritably.

'I am coming to that', said Quintilius. 'Interestingly enough Barabbas had been roused by the words of a fanatical preacher, Jesus of Nazareth.'

'What makes that interesting?', demanded Pilate.

'Jesus has himself been seized by the Sanhedrin and sent to us for execution on a charge of blasphemy.'

'Blasphemy?', said Pilate. 'I am not interested. The Jewish religion bores me. Their blasphemer can wait.'

'The Jews I have spoken to said our charge would have to be one of treason.'

'Are you saying that it would be more expedient to release the preacher?'

'That will be for Your Excellency to decide. The preacher himself appears to be harmless enough, but his preaching seems to anger violent extremists, like Barabbas. If he was released his preaching might bring more of them into the open, when we could deal with them. On the other hand the release of a blasphemer might dismay the Sanhedrin more than the release of a Zealot.'

Pilate reflected a moment. 'It is a complicated business', he said. 'In your opinion, what is the most important consideration?'

'The goodwill of Rome', answered Quintilius.

'Rome?' queried Pilate. 'What does that mean? Rome?'

'With every respect, Your Excellency, I mean that if disorders continue despite so many executions, Rome might consider Your Excellency responsible.'

Pilate wanted to lose his temper but controlled himself. 'You think Barabbas is a ringleader, and if we could use the preacher to induce a few more of the ringleaders to betray themselves, things would quieten down?'

Quintilius inclined his head.

'I will see these Jews', Pilate said. 'Send them to the trial room.'

'I regret, Your Excellency,' said Quintilius, 'that we must go out to them.'

'What?', Pilate exclaimed.

'They refuse to enter', said Quintilius. 'They are exceedingly firm. It has to do with their religious scruples. They would be defiled by entering the house of a heathen.'

'What a people!', exclaimed Pilate. 'I despise and detest the lot of them.'

He would, he decided, be in no hurry to meet these fanatical representatives of the Sanhedrin. If they wouldn't come in neither would he go out, not until it suited him. At length, however, supported by Quintilius, he made his appearance. He assumed a bored, indifferent air as though their affairs were too trivial to concern him.

'You well know,' he said, 'that I am not concerned with infractions of the law of your religion. My function is political and administrative.'

'We know that, Your Excellency', said Haggai, who was a chosen speaker for the deputation. 'But this man perverts our religion. If he were not an evil-doer we would not have brought him to you.'

'He says he is the Christ,' enlarged Zerah, 'meaning the anointed one.'

238

'Thank you', said Pilate, 'I do know some Greek.'

'The anointed state refers expressly to kingship', Haggai explained. 'Therefore in claiming to be the anointed one Jesus was claiming to be king in Israel – a claim we utterly deny.'

Pilate ignored their inferences about the anointed one. 'Has he ever incited the people to overthrow Rome?', he asked.

Haggai and Zerah were silent. They had not expected Pilate to be so difficult.

'Your silence must mean that he has *not* spoken against Rome.' He turned to Quintilius. 'He's a religious crank, Quintilius. I'm glad to have received a report on him, but I've more urgent things to do than deal with this superstitious nonsense.'

Haggai was fast losing his temper, but Zerah laid a warning hand on his arm. 'Your Excellency,' he said, 'the matter is of the utmost importance. The man has been guilty of the most frightful blasphemy, and should suffer the penalty which, under the Law of Moses, blasphemy incurs. This Jesus calls himself the Son of God. Surely Your Excellency can understand –'

'His Excellency', Quintilius broke in, 'is not interested in your religious riddles.'

'It is not a riddle', replied Zerah. 'It is a stark affront to the whole nation. The man has defiled our religion. He has affronted God.'

'My only consideration', retorted Pilate, 'is law and order. Is this man a threat to Roman order?'

'Your Excellency,' said Zerah, 'he has already broken a Roman law.'

'Which law?', demanded Pilate irritably.

'He calls himself the King of the Jews,' Zerah said.

'Has he made the claim explicitly, or is this your interpretation of something he has said about being anointed?', demanded Pilate.

'In the most explicit terms and before many witnesses, Your Excellency, he has claimed to be the King of the Jews', Zerah assured him. 'And he has told the people not to pay tribute to Caesar.'

'Ah, that would indeed be treason, would it not, Quintilius?'

'It would indeed, Your Excellency', said Quintilius.

'Very well', said Pilate. 'I will see what the man has to say for himself. Bring him to me.'

Jesus, who had been standing some way apart surrounded by guards, was now brought forward, and confronted Pilate for the first time.

Pilate looked scornfully at the deputation. 'Is this your dangerous aspirant to kingship?', he asked. 'Tattered, barefoot, emaciated.' He turned and spoke to Jesus. 'The chief priests of your Temple accuse you of leading the people astray.' Jesus remained silent. 'Of telling them not to pay tribute to the Emperor', continued Pilate. Jesus still gave no answer. 'Of claiming to be the King of Jews', Pilate persisted. 'Are you the King of the Jews?'

'If my kingdom were of this world, my men would have fought to prevent me being captured.'

'You are a king then?', said Pilate.

'Yes, I am', said Jesus. 'It was for this that I was born. I came into the world for this: to bear witness to the truth; and all who are on the side of truth listen to my voice.'

'What is truth?', said Pilate, and looked at Jesus in some perplexity. 'Who are you?', he asked.

Jesus looked into the Procurator's eyes. Hardened though Pilate was the steady gaze disturbed him. He looked away to the members of the Sanhedrin. 'I understand neither him nor his words,' he said, 'but I do understand one thing. There are no grounds for condemning him to death.'

His accusers were angered by the judgement, and made no attempt to conceal their feelings. Pilate merely called out to the guards, 'Take him away. Give him a token flogging and then let him go'.

The Roman guards marched Jesus away to a column in a far corner of the courtyard. His garments were torn off in preparation for the flogging, and other soldiers joined the group.

A Roman flogging was a fearful ordeal. It was carried out with a long leathern whip, studded at intervals with pellets of lead and sharpened pieces of bone. Quite literally, it could tear a man's back to ribbons. Men had been known to go mad under the lash, and few retained consciousness to the end.

'Nothing else, is there?', Pilate said to Quintilius as Jesus was led off.

'Well, perhaps Your Excellency should see your orders carried out', said Quintilius. So Pilate waited, chatting to Quintilius and ignoring the members of the Sanhedrin while Jesus was tied to the pillar and scourged.

Pilate had ordered a token flogging. But the officer in charge was a Syrian, and there were Syrian soldiers among those wielding the lash. As Syrians were great haters of the Jews, the men naturally put their heart into their work. At last Jesus's head was slack against the column, and the officer called the whipping to a halt. 'Enough', he said. 'Put his clothes back on.'

'But he said he was a king,' a centurion protested, 'the King of the Jews. Surely we ought to attire him as befits his rank.' He laughed and pulling a purple cloak from the nearest soldier, draped it about Jesus. Another soldier, catching the spirit of the game, disappeared for a moment and returned carrying a branch studded with long piercing thorns. He deftly twisted the branch into the shape of a crown which he placed on Jesus's head and then crushed down. 'Oughtn't he to have a sceptre?', asked the officer, grinning, and a soldier thrust a reed into Jesus's hand.

Advised that the flogging was over, Pilate was about to leave, but the voice of Zerah detained him. While Pilate had studiously ignored them the members of the Sanhedrin had conferred together. Now the voice of Zerah was respectful, but it was strong and insistent. 'Your Excellency,' it said, 'we find it hard to understand why you resist the condemnation of this man. Anyone who claims to be a king is surely speaking treason against Caesar. If you let him go will it not be said that you are no friend of Caesar? And may not a rumour get back to Caesar himself?'

Pilate paused. He was angry, but he was caught in a dilemma. He was satisfied that Jesus was politically harmless, and he had no wish to serve the religious feud of his accusers. But their veiled threats about Caesar were disturbing. His administration had not been too successful, and Caesar was only too ready to listen to damaging rumours. He had been impressed by Jesus but he was certainly not going to take risks for him. Neither was he going to give way to his fanatical accusers without a struggle. So, as though closing the issue, he said, 'It is customary to release a prisoner in celebration of the Passover. I will release this man'.

They reacted with unconcealed anger to this solution of his problem, and he again tried to outwit them. 'The people shall decide', he said. 'Let the voice of the people be heard.' And he gave orders for the crowd to be admitted to the courtyard. Then he turned to the guards and said, 'Where is he? Bring forth this King of the Jews.'

Jesus was pushed roughly forward, scarce able to stand. Pilate flinched slightly at his appearance. Blood had congealed on his forehead where the crown of thorns had pierced. The purple cloak did little to hide the terrible weals and gashes on his body. Pointing to him, Pilate turned to the crowd which had poured excitedly into the courtyard and said, 'Behold the man!'

To his surprise, for he had expected the Jews to feel sympathy for a Jewish prisoner, the crowd yelled, 'Crucify him!'

'Why, what evil has he done?', Pilate cried.

'He is a false prophet. He said he was equal to God. Crucify him.'

Jesus tood quietly amid the uproar and Pilate was astonished by his dignity. He spoke to him in a low voice. 'Who are you?', he said. 'Why don't you defend yourself? Surely you realize that I have power to crucify or to release you?'

'You would have no power over me', answered Jesus, 'if it had not been given to you from our Father in heaven.'

Pilate again turned to the crowd. 'It is the Passover,' he said, 'a time of clemency. According to a custom of yours I should release one prisoner. Shall I release this man?'

The Zealots yelled, 'No. Set free Barabbas'. Other voices in the crowd took up the cry. 'Let Barabbas go free. Barabbas. Barabbas. Barabbas.' Amidst the clamour Mary with a few others shouted desperately for Jesus, but their voices were drowned by the shouts for his rival. 'Set Jesus free,' they shouted, 'he is innocent. He is the Messiah. Release Jesus.' But the Zealots shouted still louder. 'Barabbas. Set free Barabbas. Jesus is a false prophet. Crucify him.'

'Barabbas?', Pilate shouted questioningly. The crowd roared still louder. 'Barabbas, Barabbas, Barabbas.' Pilate looked at Jesus. He stood quietly watching the crowd, giving no outward sign of anxiety or despair over his fate.

'Very well', said Pilate turning to Quintilius. 'They want Barabbas. They shall have Barabbas. What difference does it make, anyway? I'm sick of the whole business and wish I'd never seen this Jesus. Set Barabbas free.'

'And Jesus?', queried Quintilius.

'I'll sign the death warrant.'

Quintilius was also a bearer of news which he found very distasteful. He appeared in the cell where Barabbas, still shackled, was being held with Aram and Joah, and told the warder to unloose him. Then he motioned towards the open door.

'Now get out', he said disgustedly to Barabbas.

'The time has come, has it?', said Barabbas. 'Well, do your worst. I spit on Rome and its bloody might. The day of the Lord is coming and then your bloody might will go down in flame and destruction.'

'I could have you re-arrested for that,' said Quintilius, 'but I didn't hear it. Go on. Out! Order for your release. Signed by the Deputy Procurator. As for you two,' he continued, turning to Aram and Joah, 'the order's been signed for your execution.' He turned again to Barabbas who was lingering uncertainly by the warder. 'Why they let you go I'll never understand.'

At this Aram set up his usual protesting whine. 'There must be a terrible mistake', he wailed. 'I'm the innocent one here. I'm the one they meant to release, not Barabbas. I didn't do anything.' Suddenly Joah screamed at Barabbas, 'You sold yourself. That's what you did. You sold yourself to the Roman bastards'. He flung himself at the Zealot but the guards pulled him off.

'Get out before I kick you out', Quintilius shouted, and the guards dragged Barabbas through the cell door.

Pilate had retired to his own apartments. He looked moodily over the city spread out before him, and picked indifferently at his food. The interruption when Quintilius appeared was welcome.

'The Jews have been back again', Quintilius told him. 'Dissatisfied as usual. They don't approve of the board stating the Nazarene's crime that's to go up over his cross. It says "Jesus of Nazareth, King of the Jews". They say he only alleged . . .'

'What I have written,' Pilate said harshly, 'I have written.'

As part of the ritual of Roman crucifixion the prisoner was forced to carry the transverse beam of his own cross to the place of execution. Jesus, with the crown of thorns still pressing into his head, was accordingly taken to the fortress woodyard to be saddled with this crushing burden.

As he entered the yard he felt a pang of memory almost more acute than his physical sufferings. The orderly row of tools, the stacks of timber, the chippings littering the floor, the pungent-sweet smell of wood, all carried him back to the carefree days in Joseph's shop when, as a boy, he climbed the ladder and looked out at the roads that stretched to the ends of the earth. Now he was on the road that would end . . .

'That's the lot for today then?' said the carpenter.

'The third and the last,' said the officer. 'You can tie him up.' The cross beam was lifted and roped to Jesus's lacerated back. In intense pain and weakness he began the walk to Calvary.

The tragic procession had to pass under some arches that opened on to the streets of Jerusalem, close to the fortress. Nicodemus was lurking behind one of the pillars, watching with a bursting heart as Jesus dragged past. Jesus looked at him, and Nicodemus's eyes filled with tears. The recognition caused Jesus to falter for a moment, and a guard pushed him brutally forward. Nicodemus clasped his hands together and broke into uncontrollable weeping. A verse of Scripture echoed in his mind: '. . . like a lamb led to the slaughter'.

It was intensely hot. The sun scorched down from a sky that was like a dome of beaten copper. Then the murmur of a sad lament made itself heard. Nicodemus, conscious only of the tragic figure of Jesus, was reciting the prophecy of Isaiah:

'He was despised and rejected of men; a man of sorrows and acquainted with grief, and we hid as it were our faces from him. He was despised and we esteemed him not. Surely he has borne our griefs and carried our sorrows. Yet, we did esteem him, stricken, smitten of God and afflicted. But he was wounded for our transgressions. He was bruised for our iniquities. The chastisement for our sins was laid upon him, and through his wounds we are healed. We all, like sheep, have gone astray, each taking his own way. And the Lord had laid on him the iniquities of us all. He was oppressed and he was afflicted, yet he opened not his mouth. He was brought as a lamb to the slaughter and, as a sheep before its shearer is dumb, so he opens not his mouth.'

The guards, weary of the hostility of the crowd, began systematically prodding Jesus to make him move faster. At last, weak to the point of utter exhaustion, he stumbled and fell. Struggling up he shakily tried to regain his balance, but fell again. A woman emerged from the crowd and mercifully wiped the sweat and blood from his face. His sight cleared for a moment, and he gazed at her face as if to memorize its features. Then he stumbled forward once more.

At last they reached Calvary. Joah had already been fixed to his cross, and Aram, howling and screaming piteously like a wounded animal, was being nailed down. Jesus staggered up the final stretch of the way.

Aram and Joah were now erect on their crosses with a space for the third cross between. As Jesus reached the place of execution some women in dark garments were waiting for him. They were a small group of compassionate ladies who had secured the right to offer drugged wine to the condemned in order to dull the pain when the nails were hammered home. Aram and Joah had gulped down this merciful draught with frantic eagerness. Jesus asked for no stupefying drug, and gently put the cup aside.

There was a disturbance in the crowd. John and Martha, their faces drawn and pale from sleepless anguish, pushed forward to get as near to him as possible. He lay on the ground, and his hands were nailed to the cross-piece to which he was also bound. With professional expertise the soldiers had soon completed their work. Then he was hoisted up and his feet were fastened to the upright. Nicodemus, who had followed with the crowd, was still murmuring to himself. 'God so loved the world that he sent his only begotten son . . .'

Pilate's sign had gone up over the cross, 'Jesus of Nazareth, King of the Jews'. Some Pharisees pressed forward, protesting bitterly. 'It's an insult. Blasphemy. Pull down that inscription. He's not the King of the Jews.' The Roman soldiers ignored them and then, when they grew more importunate, thrust them back into the crowd.

Mary, the mother of Jesus, Martha and Mary of Magdala were trying to make their way through the crowd to the foot of the cross, but those in front were intent on mocking Jesus, and kept pushing them back.

A voice cried, 'If you are what you say you are, why don't you come down from the cross?' Another called, 'He saved others, but can't save himself.' Yet another, 'Show us a miracle. We're all waiting'.

Amid the confused noise of the crowd the jeering voices got through to Jesus. 'Father,' he prayed, 'forgive them, for they know not what they do.'

Mary had reached the front of the crowd and tried to force her way through the cordon of guards. 'I'm his mother', she pleaded. 'Let me through.'

'How can you prove it?', the sergeant asked.

The centurion whose servant Jesus had healed, shocked by what had happened, but impotent to help, stood dejectedly close by the cross. 'Let these women through', he said to the sergeant. 'She is his mother.' But when Mary Magdalene came forward he surveyed her uncertainly and asked, 'Who are you?'

'I am one of the family', she said.

He looked at the mother of Jesus and asked, 'Is that right?' She looked at Mary of Magdala, whom she had never seen before. 'Yes', she said, 'she belongs to us.'

The three women went together to the foot of the cross. The burning sun was vanishing behind a heavy, menacing cloud and the wind was rising strongly. There was a distant mutter of thunder. Some of the simpler people took this weather change as a portent. John and James the Less cautiously appeared. They too pushed their way to the cross. The centurion saw them and they shrank back in fear, but he signed them to come on. 'I remember you', he said. 'Go to him.'

Jesus looked down from the cross and saw them. 'Woman,' he said to Mary, 'behold your son,' and he looked toward John. Then he said to John, 'Behold your mother'. John put his arm round Mary, and from that moment she became his special care.

The soldiers, who had earlier been dicing, were still at the foot of the cross. Quartus, who was feeling pleased at having won, said, 'Give him something to drink'.

'No,' said Rufo, 'they don't want him to last too long. They've said the Jews can take him down before the Sabbath, because it's the Passover.'

'Never mind about orders', Quartus said obstinately. 'Pass something up on your spear.'

Then Metellus said angrily, 'I've just been having a look at these dice. They're loaded.'

'Loaded?', said Quartus. 'Honest, I didn't know. They belonged to one of those two dirty cheating bastards up there with him.'

'Oh, all right, then', Metellus said. He dipped a sponge in some wine and held it up on his spear. But Jesus turned his head aside and it was taken down again.

'*Eloi. Eloi. Lama sabachthani* . . .' said Jesus. Habakkuk and Haggai, who had gleefully joined in the taunts, overheard him. 'Nailed to a cross even now the blasphemer quotes from a psalm of David', Habakkuk exclaimed angrily. But just then he became conscious of another voice murmuring at his back. Nicodemus, gazing at Jesus, was continuing the quotation from the psalm. 'My God, my God, why hast thou forsaken me . . . I am poured out like water, and all my bones are out of joint: my heart is like wax . . . the assembly of the wicked have enclosed me: they pierced my hands and feet . . .'

Habakkuk looked uneasily up at the cross. Then he saw the soldiers with their dice. His forehead became beaded with sweat. Was it possible – were the prophecies really being fulfilled?

The voice of Nicodemus still went on, 'They part my garments among them, and cast lots for my clothes . . . But be thou not far from me, O Lord: O my strength, hasten thou to help me'.

Just then Jesus uttered an exclamation of pain. His face, contorted with the pain,

244

became suddenly calm, composed. 'Father,' he said 'into thy hands I commit my spirit.' His head fell forward. Jesus was dead.

Jesus might be dead but the problem he had created for Caiaphas was by no means at an end. The High Priest had sought audience of Pilate, and had been fortunate to catch the Procurator in the courtyard of the Antonia Fortress, thus avoiding awkward explanations about not entering a heathen dwelling.

'I know how busy you are, my dear Procurator, and shall detain you for only a moment', he began. 'I have come as a humble suitor with a simple request. At this holy Passover season we cannot have Jewish bodies left hanging on their crosses over the Sabbath. If the men who were crucified are dead, may their corpses be removed?'

'Yes', Pilate said after reflecting a moment. 'I see no objection. I'll speak to Quintilius about it. He'll give the order. We've certainly had enough of this Jesus of Nazareth, the prophet.'

'A false prophet', Caiaphas reminded him. 'And it is written in our book of Deuteronomy that "the prophet who presumes in the name of God to say things that God has not commanded, that prophet shall die".'

'Ah. I've not read the book myself,' said Pilate, 'so the force of the reference escapes me.'

Caiaphas ignored the thinly veiled sneer. 'I have a further request, Your Excellency, which concerns this false prophet, Jesus. He said – you may have heard? – that he would rise from the dead.'

'Rise from the dead!', ejaculated Pilate. 'Not after he's had a Roman spear through his heart. Why do you trouble me about such impossible nonsense?'

'I agree, my dear Procurator, that Jesus's claim to rise from the dead is impossible nonsense, as you say. Unfortunately it is the kind of impossible nonsense he dealt in; the stock in trade with which he deceived multitudes. His followers were always telling tales of the marvels and miracles he performed. And it is not at all impossible that they could steal his dead body, hide it away, and give out that he had risen from the dead and was continuing his mission in secret. Issuing orders for the foolish rabble through them.'

'You think that a serious possibility?', said Pilate. 'Well, what is it that you want me to do?'

'Let the man's burial place be guarded for a short time. From what I hear he said he would rise from the dead in three days. Three seems to have been his magical number. He said he would destroy the Temple and rebuild it in three days. A few days' watch – that's all that will be needed. His followers won't dare to approach with Roman soldiers standing by. Then the story will be discredited and his followers finished. The whole sorry business will be at an end.'

Pilate reflected again, and then shrugged. 'It all seems very far-fetched,' he said 'but I know how rumours grow.' He was about to add 'especially in this fanatical priest-ridden hole' but stopped himself in time. 'Very well,' he said, 'if you insist on guards, guards it shall be. I will give the order.'

Jesus was dead, but Mary his mother, Mary of Magdala, John, James, and Joseph of Arimathea remained in silent vigil at the foot of the cross.

A soldier who had been detailed to break the limbs of the crucified in order to hasten their death, approached the cross. As he did so Quartus called out, 'Don't bother. He's been dead for some time'.

'Orders have been received to get them down quickly', the man with the iron bar said. 'The show hasn't lasted very long this time.'

'True, but orders are orders. You can give us a hand with the unnailing', Quartus said.

Seeing these preparations for lowering the body, Joseph of Arimathea turned to Mary, the mother of Jesus. 'My family has its own burial place close to Jerusalem', he said. 'There is a tomb there where we could lay him. It is a strong tomb, carved in rock, not yet used for burial.'

Nicodemus said, 'He should be embalmed as befits his greatness. But the Sabbath will soon be starting. We shall have no time to lose. I will provide bandages and ointment.'

'I have ointment here', whispered Mary of Magdala. 'I used some of it to anoint him when he was alive.'

The storm had declined into a steady dispiriting downpour. His mother looked at his lifeless rainwashed body as the soldiers were removing it from the cross. Up to this point she had controlled herself by a more than human effort, but she now gave vent to a terrible flood of grief. The women gathered round to comfort her, while the men prepared to take up the body and carry it away for burial.

It was the morning following the Sabbath. Roman guards were posted round the rock-hewn tomb where the body of Jesus, hastily embalmed on the Friday evening, had been laid to rest. A massive boulder had been pushed into place to seal the tomb's entrance.

Zerah and another Temple official had stationed themselves a short distance apart from the soldiers, and were also keeping watch. Nothing happened the night through, then, with the dawn of Sunday scarcely breaking, they were suddenly alert. Mary Magdalene and the sisters Martha and Mary were walking timidly toward the tomb.

A sentry ordered them to halt. 'Who are you?', he demanded.

'Friends of the man who lies there', said Mary of Magdala.

'What do you want?'

'To enter the tomb.'

'Is that all?', said the sentry with heavy irony. 'Why do you want to do that?'

'To leave these herbs and spices. It is the custom.'

'Why didn't you do that when they put him in there?'

'Because the Sabbath began'. Mary explained. 'We couldn't buy these things on the Sabbath.'

'Well, perhaps you'll say how you propose to get them in now. It would take a whole squad of men to open that tomb. But you must remain here, I shall have to report you to my officer.' He prodded another soldier who, wrapped in his cloak, was sleeping on the ground. 'Here Lentullus, wake up. You're needed. Message for the officer.'

The light had become a little stronger. Only now did they become aware of two young men working in the garden on a hillock near the path leading to the tomb. One addressed the women cheerfully. 'Why do you seek the living among the dead? Jesus is risen. He is not here.'

The astonished women looked at the tomb. It was already open. The great boulder had been pushed aside. They looked back questioningly at the young man but he was no longer there.

'What's happening?' cried the bewildered sentry. Zerah and the other Temple official hurried forward, realizing with sudden alarm that the tomb was open. Bending down they entered the low doorway.

Everyone was suddenly awake. Lentullus returned with the officer, who began throwing questions at the sentry and the other guards.

He made them repeat their stories many times. 'And that's all you can tell me?', he said angrily at last. 'You were on the alert all night and heard nothing.'

'I can only speak for myself sir,' the sentry said, 'but I swear by Hercules and Jupiter . . .'

'Yes, yes,' interrupted the officer, 'I've heard all that before. You were wide awake all night long and you didn't budge from the spot.'

'That's right, sir', said the sentry. 'We were given strict instructions. Nobody's been here all night, I swear.'

'Then who moved the stone?', demanded the officer. The men remained silent. 'I don't like this,' said the officer. 'I don't like it at all, there's bound to be trouble. Are you sure you didn't play some sort of game with the thing during the night, just to pass the time?'

'Positive, sir. Those Jewish priests or whatever they are were with us all night. *They* wouldn't play games, sir.'

Zerah emerged from the tomb, panting and angry. 'There is only one explanation', he said. 'His followers came here during the night, they removed the stone.'

'Impossible', said the officer. 'I had officers posted on both sides.'

Zerah shook his head and bending down looked inside the tomb again. There was nothing. 'Now it begins,' he muttered. 'Now it all begins . . .'

As for the disciples, they had gone into hiding. John had relations who were farming not far from Jerusalem, and these sturdy folk had sheltered the disciples in one of their barns. It was a rough place but it was remote, well concealed, and seemed reasonably safe.

Their faces drawn by anxiety and grief, they huddled together round a bench which served as a table, in scarcely broken silence. When someone knocked at the door several of them visibly started. Andrew, who was nearest the door, looked at Peter, to whom they all looked for a lead, and Peter nodded his head. With his hand on the bolt Andrew softly inquired, 'Who's there?'

'Me, Philip', the voice outside replied. Andrew let him in and promptly shot the bolt again. Without speaking Philip stepped up to the table and turned out the bread and wine from the basket he was carrying.

'Did no one follow you?', asked Bartholomew.

'No. No one.'

'Are you sure?', persisted Bartholomew.

'Of course I'm sure. I took the greatest possible care.'

'Soldiers about?', queried Matthew.

'Yes, everywhere. We must get away from this place.'

'But where can we go?', asked James.

'Back to Galilee. This place is a deathtrap.'

'We must keep calm', said Peter. 'We must think what the Master would have wanted, and do that.'

Thomas shook his head disconsolately. 'The Master is dead', he said.

Suddenly there was a loud and urgent knocking at the door. They looked round startled, and in a reproachful whisper Matthew said to Philip, 'You told us you weren't followed.'

'I wasn't', retorted Philip, keeping his voice low.

Again there was a knocking at the door, louder and more insistent. They looked fearfully at one another until Peter, driven by desperation to boldness, went to the door and flung it wide open. 'Why, Mary!', he exclaimed.

Mary of Magdala came into the barn. She seemed in a strange uplifted mood, bursting with excitement yet spiritually serene.

'Peter, Matthew, all of you,' she cried, 'I've seen him!'

'Seen him?', said Matthew. 'Seen who?'

'The Master,' answered Mary, 'I've seen him. So have Martha and Mary.'

'What on earth are you talking about?', said John.

'He has risen from the dead. He's alive, here.'

'He can't be', said Thomas.

Mary reached for a stool. She was physically tired despite her excitement. 'At the tomb,' she said, 'there was a young man who seemed to be clothed in light. When we asked the soldiers for permission to take herbs and spices into the tomb he said, "Why do you look for the living among the dead? Jesus is not here. He is risen." Then we saw that the stone sealing the entrance had been moved. Martha went in. I saw the grave clothes lying on the ground. We looked for the body, but it wasn't there.'

'The soldiers must have taken it', exclaimed Andrew.

'Let her finish', Peter said.

'When we looked again for the young man', Mary continued, 'he had gone. But then I met another man. I thought he was the gardener. He saw how desperate I was and said, "Why are you weeping?" I said, "Because they have taken the body of my lord". Then he spoke my name. He said "Mary", and at once I knew. There was no mistaking him when he said that. It was Jesus. I said "Master". I fell on my knees and clung to him. He said, "Touch me not, for I have not yet ascended to my Father. Go and find the brethren and tell them." And so I came, running much of the way, for I was so excited.'

There was a silence. The disciples looked at each other, wondering and unsure, each waiting for the other to speak first. At last Thomas burst out, 'I can't believe it. I'll never believe it'.

'Do you think I'm mad?', Mary cried. 'I've seen him, I tell you, with my own eyes.'

'Why don't you go home, Mary', John said sympathetically. 'You're tired. You need a good rest.'

'You'll see him yourself', Mary cried, vexed almost to tears by their incredulity. 'You'll see him.'

248

There was an uncomfortable silence. She went to the door. Andrew let her out, firmly bolting the door again as she slipped away.

'What can you expect', Thomas said dejectedly. 'An hysterical woman.'

John looked at him thoughtfully. 'You didn't believe when he raised Jairus's daughter', he said.

'Does that mean you *do* believe her story?', demanded Thomas. He flung the question at the other disciples. 'Do you believe? Can you believe?' No one replied. Then he asked Peter yet again, '*Do* you believe?'

Peter spoke slowly, as though spelling out his thoughts. 'I think I do', he said. 'After all, it was what he predicted, but we were too frightened by what happened next to take much notice. We all failed him. I failed him worse than any of you. I denied him because I was a coward. But we all deserted him. The members of the Sanhedrin condemned him, but then they didn't know him. We did know him. We ate with him, lived with him, witnessed his mighty acts. We believed he was the Messiah, and still we betrayed him. We are more guilty than those who condemned him. But although we failed him I begin to believe that he won't fail us. He raised others from the dead. Why then should he not triumph over death himself?'

They fell silent, each puzzling over this staggering thought.

At last, something made Andrew turn and look towards the barn door. He gasped, making Peter and the others swing round too. They could hardly believe their eyes. Some of the disciples shrank back, more frightened than before, but Peter cried, 'Master!'

Jesus stood there, silhouetted against the light in the doorway.

'Why are you afraid?', Jesus asked. 'Why do you doubt me? I am here.'

Joy began to dispel the dark shadows from their faces. They were caught up in a great wave of warmth and happiness, as when old friends meet after a long absence. Matthew said, almost laughingly, 'Master, your persecutors will be confused for ever'.

More gravely, but with undiminished affection, Jesus said, 'Why were you so slow to understand? Why were your hearts troubled? Remember the words of the prophets. The Son of Man will suffer and on the third day rise from the dead, and in his name repentance for the forgiveness of sins will be preached to all the nations. Receive the Holy Spirit', he said. 'Go now like lambs among wolves.'

'Lord,' said Peter, 'stay with us, for the night is falling.'

'Do not fear', said Jesus. 'I will be with you to the end of time. And beyond.'

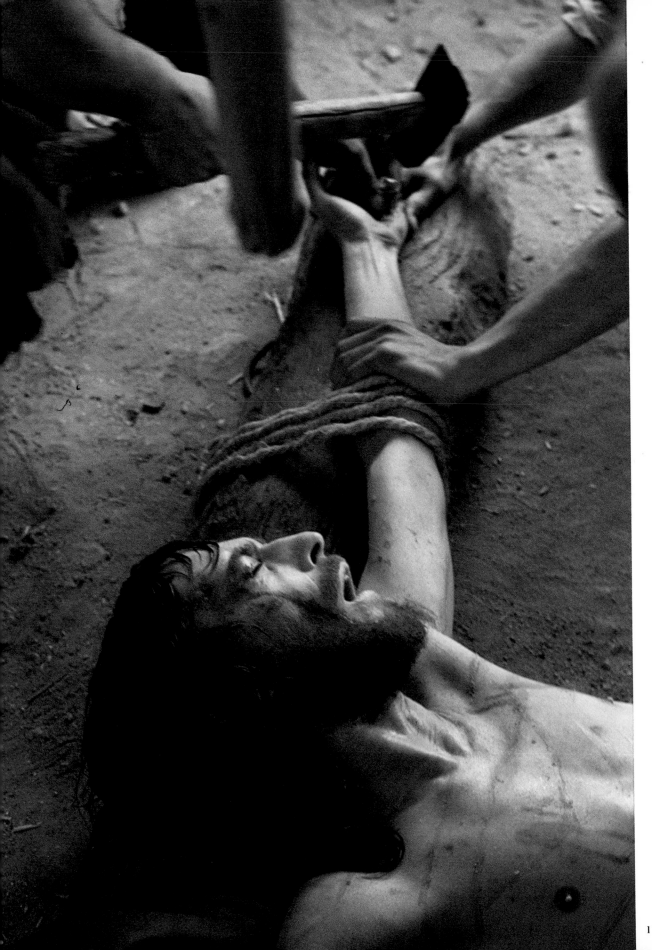

MAP

WORD LIST

PRINCIPAL
CHARACTERS

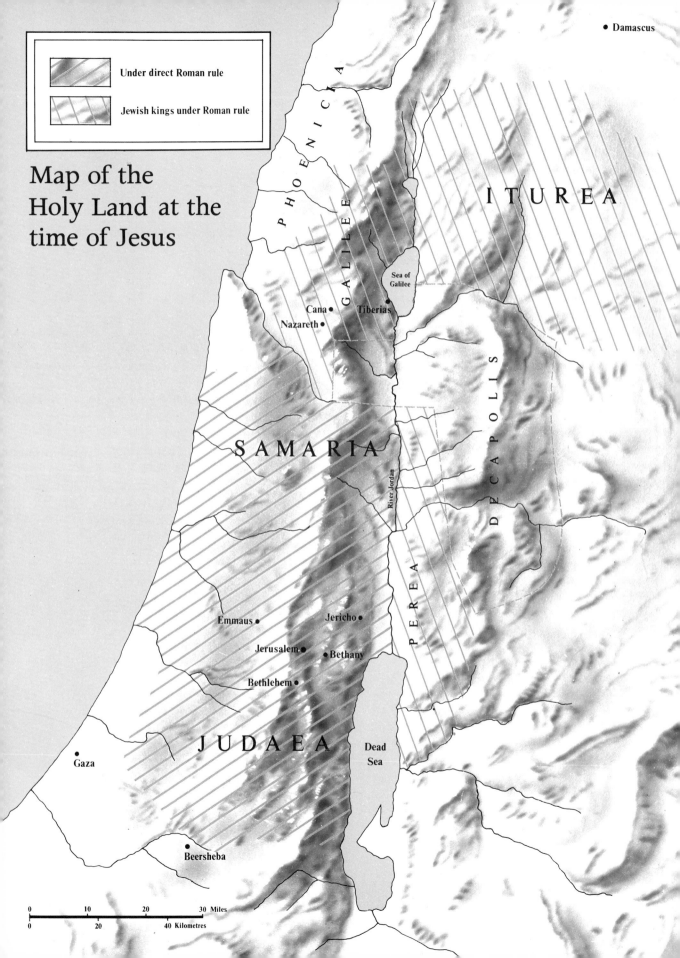

Map of the Holy Land at the time of Jesus

Under direct Roman rule

Jewish kings under Roman rule

• Damascus

PHOENICIA

GALILEE

ITUREA

Sea of Galilee

Cana •   • Tiberias

Nazareth •

SAMARIA

DECAPOLIS

River Jordan

PEREA

Emmaus •   Jericho •

Jerusalem •   • Bethany

Bethlehem •

JUDAEA

Dead Sea

• Gaza

• Beersheba

| 0 | 10 | 20 | 30 Miles |
| 0 | 20 | 40 Kilometres | |

Word List

and historical background

THE LAW

The word 'law' as used in the Bible has three different meanings.

1. There is its basic meaning, which is the Ten Commandments.
2. It means the first five books of the Old Testament, the books we call the Pentateuch or the Five Rolls – Genesis, Exodus, Leviticus, Numbers, Deuteronomy.
3. There is the meaning of oral law, and for New Testament understanding this is probably the most important of the three.

The oral law was never written down, but was passed from mouth to mouth throughout the generations. It came from the fact that it was a conviction of the Jew that the Law was perfect, and if it was perfect it must be complete. It must therefore be possible to extract from it a rule or regulation for every possible man in every possible situation in life. Take for instance the Sabbath law.

The Sabbath law forbade work on the Sabbath day. But you may well ask, what is work? To take one example, a man was forbidden to carry a burden on the Sabbath day (Jeremiah 17:21). But we may well ask then, what is a burden? And so we have to ask, if a woman goes out with a brooch on her dress, is she carrying a burden? If she goes out with some false hair, is she carrying a burden? If a man has a wooden leg, is he carrying a burden? If he has artificial dentures, is he carrying a burden? So oral law goes on to define what a burden is in pages of definition, of which one example is anything that weighs as much as two dried figs.

Now this process is endless, but this is the process which the most devout people of the Jews carried on in the time of Jesus. The most devout people were the **Pharisees**. The Pharisees literally mean 'the separated ones'. They had separated themselves from all the ordinary activities of life to obey the many regulations of the scribal and the oral law. There were never more than 6000 of them, and they were the fine flower of Jewish piety. But if they were right, Jesus was wrong, because Jesus did not believe in hundreds and hundreds of little rules and regulations. He believed in love for God and love for our fellow men, and it is easy to see how the Pharisees felt that Jesus was destroying religion.

Along with the Pharisees, we usually mention the **Sadducees**, but the Sadducees and the Pharisees were very different. The Sadducees did not accept the oral law. They did not go beyond the written law. Further, there were not many Sadducees, but those there were, were aristocratic and wealthy. Because they were aristocratic and wealthy, they were the collaborationist party. They wanted to stand well with the Romans in order to keep their privileges, their wealth and their luxurious way of living. Therefore, the last kind of person they wanted was a Messiah. They did not want the status quo disturbed in the least. Most of the priests were Sadducees.

When we speak of the Pharisees and the Sadducees we think of the **Sanhedrin**, which was the governing body of the Jews. It was composed of Pharisees, Sadducees and Elders. The **Elders** were, so to speak, the lay section of the council. The **High Priest** was the president of the Sanhedrin and presided over its deliberations and its decisions. It had 70 members. At one time the Sanhedrin could have inflicted the death penalty by itself, but in the time of Jesus Palestine was an occupied and subject country, and therefore, although the Sanhedrin could demand the death penalty, it could not inflict it. This had to be done by the Romans.

Still thinking of the law, another set of people we think of are the **Scribes**. The Scribes were the experts in law. They did not necessarily keep the law in all its detail as Pharisees did, but they knew the detail and they were the experts. The greatest of the Scribes had the title **'Rabbi'**, which means 'my great one'.

MARRIAGE LAW

Marriage law in Palestine was unique in one thing. When two people became betrothed, the betrothal lasted for one year. During that year they were treated as if they were married and the betrothal could not be broken by any other means than by divorce. The betrothal was just as binding as the marriage. That is why Joseph contemplated divorcing Mary even before they were married, until he understood what had happened to her.

MESSIAH

The word 'Messiah' and the word 'Christ' are the same. Messiah is the Hebrew for 'anointed', Christ is the Greek for it, and the Messiah or the Christ is God's anointed king of his people. He is the king specially sent by God to lead and liberate the Jewish nation.

PALESTINE

Palestine was a small country. It was only about 120 miles from north to south and it was less than 50 miles from east to west. It is further from Glasgow to Edinburgh or from New York to Philadelphia than across the whole of Palestine. Palestine was composed of three parts.

In the north there was **Galilee,** round the Sea of Galilee. Galilee was not much more than 50 miles from north to south and 25 miles from east to west, but it was an extraordinarily populous part of the country because it was extraordinarily fertile. Josephus tells us that in Galilee there were 204 villages, none of which had a population of fewer than 15,000. We need not accept this as literally true, although Josephus was Governor of Galilee for a time, but it does show us the enormous population that lived there. Proceeding south, the next bit of Palestine was **Samaria**. The Samaritans had a constant feud with the Jews. The Jews had no dealings with the Samaritans. Further south there was **Judea**, with the capital city of Jerusalem. Galilee was much the most progressive part of Palestine. It was on the road to everywhere, for the great roads from Egypt to Damascus and from Acre to the Far East passed through it, whereas Judea was on the way to nowhere. It was a backwater and therefore felt none of the moving impulses that Galilee must have felt. It is significant that Jesus's greatest successes were in Galilee.

THE PASSOVER

The Passover was the greatest festival of the Jewish year. It took place in mid-April and it commemorated the escape of the Jewish people from slavery in Egypt. The name comes from the fact that the last of the plagues to strike Egypt was the death of the first-born in every household. The lintels of the Jewish households were marked with the blood of the lamb, so that the angel of death would recognize that it was a Jew who lived there and not carry out his deadly work in that house.

THE ROMANS IN PALESTINE

Palestine was not a Roman province, but was part of the province of Syria. It was too large to be a district and too small to be a province. It therefore had a special kind of governor, called a **Procurator**. This was what Pilate was. He was in charge of Palestine, but he was subordinate to, and answerable to, the Governor of Syria. Palestine was troubled country, especially due to the fact that the **Zealots** were strong. The Zealots were violent nationalists and were pledged to the destruction of the Romans, even by murder and assassination. They were by far the most violent nationalists in Palestine.

Principal characters featured in the photographs

Jesus as a man	ROBERT POWELL
Jesus as a boy	LORENZO MONET
Yehuda the Rabbi	CYRIL CUSACK
Herod the Great	PETER USTINOV
Proculus	ROBERT BEATTY
Saturninus	NORMAN BOWLER
Naso	JOHN PHILLIPS
Joseph	YORGO VOYAGIS
Mary	OLIVIA HUSSEY
Elizabeth	MARINA BERTI
Anna	REGINA BIANCHI
Abigail	NANCY NEVISON
The Shepherds:	JONATHAN ADAMS
	ROY HOLDER
	RENATO TERRA
Simeon	RALPH RICHARDSON
The Magi:	
Gaspar	FERNANDO REY
Melchior	DONALD PLEASENCE
Balthazar	JAMES EARL JONES
John the Baptist	MICHAEL YORK
Herod Antipas	CHRISTOPHER PLUMMER
Herodias	VALENTINA CORTESE
Mad boy	KEITH SKINNER
Salome	ISABEL MESTRES
Mary of Magdala	ANNE BANCROFT
Joseph of Arimathea	JAMES MASON
The Adulteress	CLAUDIA CARDINALE
Simon the Pharisee	FRANCIS DE WOLFE

The Zealots:

Amos	IAN BANNEN
Joel	OLIVER TOBIAS
Hosias	GEORGE CAMILLER
Saul	OLIVER SMITH
Daniel	ROBERT DAVEY

The Apostles:

Simon Peter	JAMES FARENTINO
Andrew his brother	TONY VOGEL
James the son of Zebedee	JONATHAN MULLER
John his brother	JOHN DUTTINE
Philip	STEVE GARDNER
Bartholomew	JOHN EASTHAM
Thomas	BRUCE LIDINGTON
Matthew the tax-collector	KEITH WASHINGTON
James the son of Alphaeus	SERGIO NICOLAI
Thaddeus	MIMMO CRAO
Simon the Zealot	MURRAY SALEM
Judas Iscariot	IAN MCSHANE

Martha	MARIA CARTA
Zerah	IAN HOLM
Barabbas	STACY KEACH
The centurion	ERNEST BORGNINE
The blind man	RENATO RASCEL
Caiaphas	ANTHONY QUINN
Habbakuk	LEE MONTAGUE
Nicodemus	LAURENCE OLIVIER
Pontius Pilate	ROD STEIGER
Quintillius	TONY LO BIANCO

Director of the film	FRANCO ZEFFIRELLI
Produced by	VINCENZO LABELLA
Executive Producer	BERNARD J. KINGHAM
Associate Producer	DYSON LOVELL
Music composed and conducted by	MAURICE JARRE

Distributed throughout the world by